Representing Time

Timelines and Rhythm Patterns

Grade 2

Also appropriate for Grade 3

Tracey Wright
Ricardo Nemirovsky
Cornelia Tierney

Developed at TERC, Cambridge, Massachusetts

Dale Seymour Publications®
White Plains, New York

The *Investigations* curriculum was developed at TERC (formerly
Technical Education Research Centers) in collaboration with Kent State
University and the State University of New York at Buffalo. The work was
supported in part by National Science Foundation Grant No. ESI-9050210.
TERC is a nonprofit company working to improve mathematics and science
education. TERC is located at 2067 Massachusetts Avenue, Cambridge,
MA 02140.

**This project was supported, in part,
by the**

National Science Foundation

Opinions expressed are those of the authors
and not necessarily those of the Foundation

Managing Editor: Catherine Anderson

Grade-Level Editor: Alison Abrohms

Series Editor: Beverly Cory

Revision Team: Laura Marshall Alavosus, Ellen Harding, Patty Green Holubar,
Suzanne Knott, Beverly Hersh Lozoff

ESL Consultant: Nancy Sokol Green

Production/Manufacturing Director: Janet Yearian

Production/Manufacturing Coordinator: Amy Changar, Shannon Miller

Design Manager: Jeff Kelly

Design: Don Taka

Illustrations: Laurie Harden, Meryl Treatner

Cover: Bay Graphics

Composition: Archetype Book Composition

This book is published by Dale Seymour Publications®, an imprint of
Addison Wesley Longman, Inc.

Dale Seymour Publications
10 Bank Street
White Plains, NY 10602
Customer Service 1-800-872-1100

Order number DS43807
ISBN 1-57232-660-3
6 7 8 9 10-ML-02 01 00

Printed on Recycled Paper

T E R C

CONTENTS

TEACHER NOTES

WHERE TO START

The first-time user of *Timelines and Rhythm Patterns* should read the following:

When you next teach this same unit, you can begin to read more of the background. Each time you present the unit, you will learn more about how your students understand the mathematical ideas.

Investigations in Number, Data, and Space® is a K–5 mathematics curriculum with four major goals:

- to offer students meaningful mathematical problems
- to emphasize depth in mathematical thinking rather than superficial exposure to a series of fragmented topics
- to communicate mathematics content and pedagogy to teachers
- to substantially expand the pool of mathematically literate students

The *Investigations* curriculum embodies a new approach based on years of research about how children learn mathematics. Each grade level consists of a set of separate units, each offering 2–8 weeks of work. These units of study are presented through investigations that involve students in the exploration of major mathematical ideas.

Approaching the mathematics content through investigations helps students develop flexibility and confidence in approaching problems, fluency in using mathematical skills and tools to solve problems, and proficiency in evaluating their solutions. Students also build a repertoire of ways to communicate about their mathematical thinking, while their enjoyment and appreciation of mathematics grows.

The investigations are carefully designed to invite all students into mathematics—girls and boys, members of diverse cultural, ethnic, and language groups, and students with different strengths and interests. Problem contexts often call on students to share experiences from their family, culture, or community. The curriculum eliminates barriers—such as work in isolation from peers, or emphasis on speed and memorization—that exclude some students from participating successfully in mathematics. The following aspects of the curriculum ensure that all students are included in significant mathematics learning:

- Students spend time exploring problems in depth.
- They find more than one solution to many of the problems they work on.

- They invent their own strategies and approaches, rather than rely on memorized procedures.
- They choose from a variety of concrete materials and appropriate technology, including calculators, as a natural part of their everyday mathematical work.
- They express their mathematical thinking through drawing, writing, and talking.
- They work in a variety of groupings—as a whole class, individually, in pairs, and in small groups.
- They move around the classroom as they explore the mathematics in their environment and talk with their peers.

While reading and other language activities are typically given a great deal of time and emphasis in elementary classrooms, mathematics often does not get the time it needs. If students are to experience mathematics in depth, they must have enough time to become engaged in real mathematical problems. We believe that a minimum of 5 hours of mathematics classroom time a week—about an hour a day—is critical at the elementary level. The scope and pacing of the *Investigations* curriculum are based on that belief.

We explain more about the pedagogy and principles that underlie these investigations in Teacher Notes throughout the units. For correlations of the curriculum to the NCTM Standards and further help in using this research-based program for teaching mathematics, see the following books, available from Dale Seymour Publications:

- *Implementing the* Investigations in Number, Data, and Space® *Curriculum*
- *Beyond Arithmetic: Changing Mathematics in the Elementary Classroom* by Jan Mokros, Susan Jo Russell, and Karen Economopoulos

This book is one of the curriculum units for *Investigations in Number, Data, and Space*. In addition to providing part of a complete mathematics curriculum for your students, this unit offers information to support your own professional development. You, the teacher, are the person who will make this curriculum come alive in the classroom; the book for each unit is your main support system.

Although the curriculum does not include student textbooks, reproducible sheets for student work are provided in the unit and are also available as Student Activity Booklets. Students work actively with objects and experiences in their own environment and with a variety of manipulative materials and technology, rather than with a book of instruction and problems. We strongly recommend use of the overhead projector as a way to present problems, to focus group discussion, and to help students share ideas and strategies.

Ultimately, every teacher will use these investigations in ways that make sense for his or her

particular style, the particular group of students, and the constraints and supports of a particular school environment. Each unit offers information and guidance for a wide variety of situations, drawn from our collaborations with many teachers and students over many years. Our goal in this book is to help you, a professional educator, implement this curriculum in a way that will give all your students access to mathematical power.

Investigation Format

The opening two pages of each investigation help you get ready for the work that follows.

What Happens This gives a synopsis of each session or block of sessions.

Mathematical Emphasis This lists the most important ideas and processes students will encounter in this investigation.

What to Plan Ahead of Time These lists alert you to materials to gather, sheets to duplicate, transparencies to make, and anything else you need to do before starting.

INVESTIGATION 1

Timelines

What Happens

Sessions 1 and 2: What Is a Timeline? As a class, students assemble a timeline about the life of Dr. Seuss and discuss the important events in his life. For homework, students collect information about key events in their own lives.

Session 3: Timeline of My Life Students create timelines of their lives using information they collected for homework. They figure out where their significant life events belong and then compare their timelines. For homework, students plan a special day, deciding which activities they would like to do in the morning, afternoon, and evening.

Sessions 4 and 5: Special Day Timelines Students brainstorm activities for a special day. In pairs, they create a timeline of a special day and play a guessing game, Secret Timelines, figuring out where another pair's activities fit in a day.

Session 6: Acting Out Timelines In pairs, students compare the time it takes to do various activities within their own special days. Students act out their Special Day Timelines by performing their daily activities on a time scale much shorter than a day.

Mathematical Emphasis

- Sequencing events
- Representing events in time
- Comparing durations of time within a day
- Developing familiarity with time notation

What to Plan Ahead of Time

Materials

- Student math folders (Sessions 1–2)
- *Miss Rumphius* by Barbara Cooney (Sessions 1–2, optional)
- Counters such as interlocking cubes, buttons, 100 chart (Sessions 1–2, optional)
- Chart paper (Sessions 1–2)
- Adding machine tape: 3–5 rolls (Sessions 1–2)
- Crayons or markers (Sessions 3–5)
- Scissors (Sessions 4–5)
- Timer (Sessions 4–5, optional)
- Analog clock (Sessions 4–5, optional)
- Digital clock (Sessions 4–5, optional)
- Paste or glue sticks (Sessions 4–5)

Continued on next page

INVESTIGATION 1

What to Plan Ahead of Time *(continued)*

Other Preparation

- Duplicate student sheets and teaching resources (located at the end of this unit) in the following quantities. If you have Student Activity Booklets, copy only the items marked with an asterisk, including any extra materials needed.

  For Sessions 1–2
  Family letter* (p. 76): 1 per student. Remember to sign and date the letter before copying it.
  Student Sheet 1, Weekly Log (p. 77): 1 per student. At this time, you may wish to duplicate a supply to last for the entire unit and distribute the sheets as needed.
  Dr. Seuss Timeline* (p. 85): 1 set for the class. Cut out the strips on each page.
  Student Sheet 2, Life Timelines (p. 78): 1 per student (homework). If possible, send this sheet home with each student before you begin the unit so that students have two nights to complete the homework.

  For Session 3
  Student Sheet 3, Special Day Activities (p. 79): 1 per student (homework)

  For Sessions 4–5
  Student Sheets 4 and 5, Special Day Timeline (pp. 80–81): 2 of each per pair, plus extras* for display
  Student Sheet 6, Events in an Adult's Life (p. 82): 1 per student (homework)

  For Session 6
  Student Sheet 7, Time Information About My Special Day (p. 83): 1 per pair
  Student Sheet 8, Special Day Stories (p. 84): 1 per student (homework)

- Prepare a math folder for each student if you did not do so for a previous unit. (Sessions 1–2)

- *Miss Rumphius* by Barbara Cooney is used in this session. If that book is not available, select a biography to read aloud. (Sessions 1–2)

- Prepare a sample timeline by folding a strip of 4-foot-long adding machine tape in half end to end, four times. Write BORN at the left edge and then write 1 at the first fold. Continue writing the years on the folds until you reach 8. See Planning Your Timeline (p. 14) for an illustration. (Session 3)

- Cut apart adding machine tape into strips about 4' long. Cut 1 per student plus several extras. Students older than 8 can add a 6" section to their timeline for each additional year. (Session 3)

- Prepare a sample of the Special Day Timeline by cutting apart a copy of Student Sheets 4 and 5 and gluing them together in order. Plan a place where you can display this timeline at a height within students' reach. (Sessions 4–5)

- Arrange a space in your classroom that is large enough for five to six students to perform their Special Day Timelines at one time. (Session 6)

Sessions Within an investigation, the activities are organized by class session, a session being at least a one-hour math class. Sessions are numbered consecutively through an investigation. Often several sessions are grouped together, presenting a block of activities with a single major focus.

When you find a block of sessions presented together—for example, Sessions 1, 2, and 3—read through the entire block first to understand the overall flow and sequence of the activities. Make some preliminary decisions about how you will divide the activities into three sessions for your class, based on what you know about your students. You may need to modify your initial plans as you progress through the activities, and you may want to make notes in the margins of the pages as reminders for the next time you use the unit.

Be sure to read the Session Follow-Up section at the end of the session block to see what homework assignments and extensions are suggested as you make your initial plans.

While you may be used to a curriculum that tells you exactly what each class session should cover, we have found that the teacher is in a better position to make these decisions. Each unit is flexible and may be handled somewhat differently by every teacher. Although we provide guidance for how many sessions a particular group of activities is likely to need, we want you to be active in determining an appropriate pace and the best transition points for your class. It is not unusual for a teacher to spend more or less time than is proposed for the activities.

Classroom Routines The Start-Up at the beginning of each session offers suggestions for how to acknowledge and integrate homework from the previous session, and which Classroom Routine activities to include sometime during the school day. Routines provide students with regular practice in important mathematical skills such as solving number combinations, collecting and organizing data, understanding time, and seeing spatial relationships. Two routines, How Many Pockets? and Today's Number, are used regularly in the grade 2 *Investigations* units. A third routine, Time and Time Again, appears in the final unit, *Timelines and Rhythm Patterns*. This routine provides a variety of activities about understanding

---

Session 3

Timeline of My Life

Materials

- Student Sheet 2 (completed homework)
- Prepared sample timeline
- Strips of adding machine tape (1 per student, plus extra tape)
- Crayons or markers
- Student Sheet 3 (1 per student, homework)

What Happens

Students create timelines of their lives using information they collected for homework. They figure out where their significant life events belong and then compare their timelines. For homework, students plan a special day, deciding which activities they would like to do in the morning, afternoon, and evening. Their work focuses on:

- working with a scale that has regular intervals
- representing significant life events along an axis of time
- marking discrete landmarks along the continuous axis of time

Start-Up

Today's Number

- **Calendar Date** If you are using the calendar date for Today's Number, brainstorm with students ways to express the number. Suggest that students include subtraction as a way to express the number. Record their expressions on chart paper so that they can be saved each day.
- **Number of School Days** If you are using the number of school days as Today's Number, and the number is over 100, encourage students to focus on ways to make 100 using multiples of 5 and 10. For example, if the number is 162, one solution is 50 + 25 + 25 + 25 + 10 + 10 + 10 + 5 + 2. Add a card to the class counting strip and fill in another number on the blank 200 chart.

For complete details on this routine, see p. 64.

Activity

Planning Your Timeline

Students will need their list of important events that they completed for homework (Student Sheet 2). Invite a few students to share an interesting item from their lists with the class. Write each event on the chalkboard along with the student's name and age. This information will be used later in the activity.

Now you know about how old you were when you did certain things in your life. But it might be hard to see on your homework list which important event happened first, which happened next, and which happened most recently. In the last math class, you put together a timeline of the important events in Dr. Seuss's life. Today you are going to be making timelines so that you can easily see the order of the important events in your life.

14 ■ *Investigation 1: Timelines*

---

time; these can be easily integrated throughout the school day and into other parts of the classroom curriculum. A fourth routine, Quick Images, supports work in the unit *Shapes, Halves, and Symmetry.* After its introduction, you might do it once or twice a week to develop students' visual sense of number (as displayed in dot arrangements).

Most Classroom Routine activities are short and can be done whenever you have a spare 10 minutes—maybe before lunch or recess, or at the beginning or end of the day. Complete descriptions of the Classroom Routines can be found at the end of the units.

Activities The activities include pair and small-group work, individual tasks, and whole-class discussions. In any case, students are seated together, talking and sharing ideas during all work times. Students most often work cooperatively, although each student may record work individually.

Choice Time In most units, some sessions are structured with activity choices. In these cases, students may work simultaneously on different activities focused on the same mathematical ideas.

Students choose which activities they want to do, and they cycle through them.

You will need to decide how to set up and introduce these activities and how to let students make their choices. Some teachers set up choices as stations around the room, while others post the list of available choices and allow students to collect their own materials and choose their own work space. You may need to experiment with a few different structures before finding a set up that works best for you, your students, and your classroom.

Tips for the Linguistically Diverse Classroom At strategic points in each unit, you will find concrete suggestions for simple modifications of the teaching strategies to encourage the participation of all students. Many of these tips offer alternative ways to elicit critical thinking from students at varying levels of English proficiency, as well as from other students who find it difficult to verbalize their thinking.

The tips are supported by suggestions for specific vocabulary work to help ensure that all students can participate fully in the investigations. The Preview for the Linguistically Diverse Classroom lists important words that are assumed as part of the working vocabulary of the unit. Second-language learners will need to become familiar with these words in order to understand the problems and activities they will be doing. These terms can be incorporated into students' second-language work before or during the unit. Activities that can be used to present the words are found in the appendix, Vocabulary Support for Second-Language Learners. In addition, ideas for making connections to students' languages and cultures, included on the Preview page, help the class explore the unit's concepts from a multicultural perspective.

Session Follow-Up: Homework In *Investigations,* homework is an extension of classroom work. Sometimes it offers review and practice of work done in class, sometimes preparation for upcoming activities, and sometimes numerical practice that revisits work in earlier units. Homework plays a role both in supporting students' learning and in helping inform families about the ways in which students in this curriculum work with mathematical ideas.

Depending on your school's homework policies and your own judgment, you may want to assign more homework than is suggested in the units. For this purpose you might use the practice pages, included as blackline masters at the end of this unit, to give students additional work with numbers.

For some homework assignments, you will want to adapt the activity to meet the needs of a variety of students in your class: those with special needs, those ready for more challenge, and second-language learners. You might change the numbers in a problem, make the activity more or less complex, or go through a sample activity with those who need extra help. You can modify any student sheet for either homework or class use. In particular, making numbers in a problem smaller or larger can make the same basic activity appropriate for a wider range of students.

Another issue to consider is how to handle the homework that students bring back to class—how to recognize the work they have done at home without spending too much time on it. Some teachers hold a short group discussion of different approaches to the assignment; others ask students to share and discuss their work with a neighbor; still others post the homework around the room

and give students time to tour it briefly. If you want to keep track of homework students bring in, be sure it ends up in a designated place.

Session Follow-Up: Extensions Sometimes in Session Follow-Up, you will find suggested extension activities. These are opportunities for some or all students to explore a topic in greater depth or in a different context. They are not designed for "fast" students; mathematics is a multifaceted discipline, and different students will want to go further in different investigations. Look for and encourage the sparks of interest and enthusiasm you see in your students, and use the extensions to help them pursue these interests.

Excursions Some of the *Investigations* units include excursions—blocks of activities that could be omitted without harming the integrity of the unit. This is one way of dealing with the great depth and variety of elementary mathematics—much more than a class has time to explore in any one year. Excursions give you the flexibility to make different choices from year to year, doing the excursion in one unit this time, and next year trying another excursion.

Materials

A complete list of the materials needed for teaching this unit follows the unit overview. Some of these materials are available in kits for the *Investigations* curriculum. Individual items can also be purchased from school supply dealers.

Classroom Materials In an active mathematics classroom, certain basic materials should be available at all times: interlocking cubes, pencils, unlined paper, graph paper, calculators, and things to count with. Some activities in this curriculum require scissors and glue sticks or tape. Stick-on notes and large paper are also useful materials throughout.

So that students can independently get what they need at any time, they should know where these materials are kept, how they are stored, and how they are to be returned to the storage area. Many teachers have found that stopping 5 minutes before the end of each session so that students can finish their work and clean up is helpful in maintaining classroom materials. You'll find that establishing such routines at the beginning of the year is well worth the time and effort.

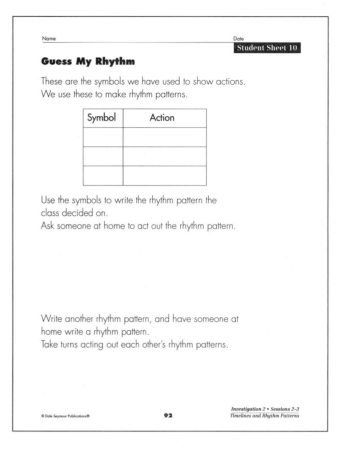

Student Sheets and Teaching Resources Student recording sheets and other teaching tools needed for both class and homework are provided as reproducible blackline masters at the end of each unit.

We think it's important that students find their own ways of organizing and recording their work. They need to learn how to explain their thinking with both drawings and written words, and how to organize their results so someone else can understand them. For this reason, we deliberately do not provide student sheets for every activity. Regardless of the form in which students do their work, we recommend that they keep their work in a mathematics folder, notebook, or journal so that it is always available to them for reference.

Student Activity Booklets These booklets contain all the sheets each student will need for individual work, freeing you from extensive copying (although you may need or want to copy the occasional teaching resource on transparency film or card stock, or make extra copies of a student sheet).

Computers and Calculators Calculators are introduced to students in the second unit of the grade 2 sequence, *Coins, Coupons, and Combinations*. It is assumed that calculators are readily available throughout the curriculum.

Computer activities are offered at all grade levels. Although the software is linked to activities in three units in grade 2, we recommend that students use it throughout the year. As students use the software over time, they continue to develop skills presented in the units. How you incorporate the computer activities into your curriculum depends on the number of computers you have available. Technology in the Curriculum discusses ways to incorporate the use of calculators and computers into classroom activities.

Children's Literature Each unit offers a list of related children's literature that can be used to support the mathematical ideas in the unit. Sometimes an activity is based on a selected children's book, with suggestions for substitutions where practical. While such activities can be adapted and taught without the book, the literature offers a rich introduction and should be used whenever possible.

Investigations **at Home** It is a good idea to make your policy on homework explicit to both students and their families when you begin teaching with *Investigations*. How frequently will you be assigning homework? When do you expect homework to be completed and brought back to school? What are your goals in assigning homework? How independent should families expect their children to be? What should the parent's or guardian's role be? The more explicit you can be about your expectations, the better the homework experience will be for everyone.

Investigations at Home (a booklet available separately for each unit, to send home with students) gives you a way to communicate with families about the work students are doing in class. This booklet includes a brief description of every session, a list of the mathematics content emphasized in each investigation, and a discussion of each homework assignment to help families more effectively support their children. Whether or not you are using the *Investigations* at Home booklets, we

expect you to make your own choices about homework assignments. Feel free to omit any and to add extra ones you think are appropriate.

Family Letter A letter that you can send home to students' families is included with the blackline masters for each unit. Families need to be informed about the mathematics work in your classroom; they should be encouraged to participate in and support their children's work. A reminder to send home the letter for each unit appears in one of the early investigations. These letters are also available separately in Spanish, Vietnamese, Cantonese, Hmong, and Cambodian.

Help for You, the Teacher

Because we believe strongly that a new curriculum must help teachers think in new ways about mathematics and about their students' mathematical thinking processes, we have included a great deal of material to help you learn more about both.

About the Mathematics in This Unit This introductory section summarizes the critical informa-

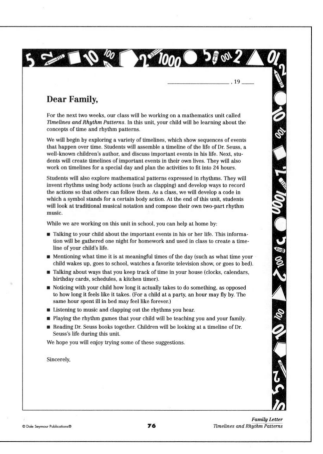

tion about the mathematics you will be teaching. It describes the unit's central mathematical ideas and the ways students will encounter them through the unit's activities.

About the Assessment in This Unit This introductory section highlights Teacher Checkpoints and assessment activities contained in the unit. It offers questions to stimulate your assessment as you observe the development of students' mathematical thinking and learning.

Teacher Notes These reference notes provide practical information about the mathematics you are teaching and about our experience with how students learn. Many of the notes were written in response to actual questions from teachers or to discuss important things we saw happening in the field-test classrooms. Some teachers like to read them all before starting the unit, then review them as they come up in particular investigations.

Dialogue Boxes Sample dialogues demonstrate how students typically express their mathematical ideas, what issues and confusions arise in their thinking, and how some teachers have guided class discussions.

These dialogues are based on the extensive classroom testing of this curriculum; many are word-for-word transcriptions of recorded class discussions. They are not always easy reading; sometimes it may take some effort to unravel what the students are trying to say. But this is the value of these dialogues; they offer good clues to how your students may develop and express their approaches and strategies, helping you prepare for your own class discussions.

Where to Start You may not have time to read everything the first time you use this unit. As a first-time user, you will likely focus on understanding the activities and working them out with your students. Read completely through all the activities before starting to present them. Also read those sections listed in the Contents under the heading Where to Start.

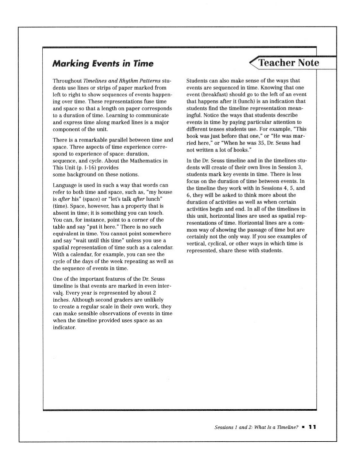

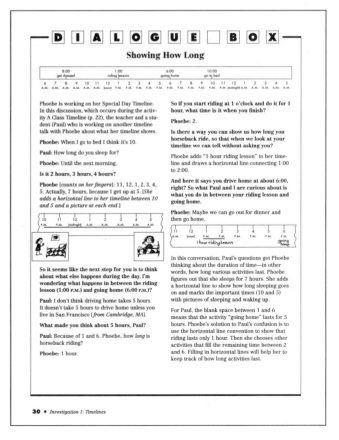

The *Investigations* curriculum incorporates the use of two forms of technology in the classroom: calculators and computers. Calculators are assumed to be standard classroom materials, available for student use in any unit. Computers are explicitly linked to one or more units at each grade level; they are used with the unit on 2-D geometry at each grade, as well as with some of the units on measuring, data, and changes.

Using Calculators

In this curriculum, calculators are considered tools for doing mathematics, similar to pattern blocks or interlocking cubes. Just as with other tools, students must learn both *how* to use calculators correctly and *when* they are appropriate to use. This knowledge is crucial for daily life, as calculators are now a standard way of handling numerical operations, both at work and at home.

Using a calculator correctly is not a simple task; it depends on a good knowledge of the four operations and of the number system, so that students can select suitable calculations and also determine what a reasonable result would be. These skills are the basis of any work with numbers, whether or not a calculator is involved.

Unfortunately, calculators are often seen as tools to check computations with, as if other methods are somehow more fallible. Students need to understand that any computational method can be used to check any other; it's just as easy to make a mistake on the calculator as it is to make a mistake on paper or with mental arithmetic. Throughout this curriculum, we encourage students to solve computation problems in more than one way in order to double-check their accuracy. We present mental arithmetic, paper-and-pencil computation, and calculators as three possible approaches.

In this curriculum we also recognize that, despite their importance, calculators are not always appropriate in mathematics instruction. Like any tools, calculators are useful for some tasks but not for others. You will need to make decisions about when to allow students access to calculators and when to ask that they solve problems without them so that they can concentrate on other tools and skills. At times when calculators are or are not appropriate for a particular activity, we make specific recommendations. Help your students develop their own sense of which problems they can tackle with their own reasoning and which ones might be better solved with a combination of their own reasoning and the calculator.

Managing calculators in your classroom so that they are a tool, and not a distraction, requires some planning. When calculators are first introduced, students often want to use them for everything, even problems that can be solved quite simply by other methods. However, once the novelty wears off, students are just as interested in developing their own strategies, especially when these strategies are emphasized and valued in the classroom. Over time, students will come to recognize the ease and value of solving problems mentally, with paper and pencil, or with manipulatives, while also understanding the power of the calculator to facilitate work with larger numbers.

Experience shows that if calculators are available only occasionally, students become excited and distracted when they are permitted to use them. They focus on the tool rather than on the mathematics. In order to learn when calculators are appropriate and when they are not, students must have easy access to them and use them routinely in their work.

If you have a calculator for each student, and if you think your students can accept the responsibility, you might allow them to keep their calculators with the rest of their individual materials, at least for the first few weeks of school. Alternatively, you might store them in boxes on a shelf, number each calculator, and assign a corresponding number to each student. This system can give students a sense of ownership while also helping you keep track of the calculators.

Using Computers

Students can use computers to approach and visualize mathematical situations in new ways. The computer allows students to construct and manipulate geometric shapes, see objects move according to rules they specify, and turn, flip, and repeat a pattern.

This curriculum calls for computers in units where they are a particularly effective tool for learning mathematics content. One unit on 2-D geometry at each of the grades 3–5 includes a core of activities that rely on access to computers, either in the classroom or in a lab. Other units on geometry, measuring, data, and changes include computer activities, but can be taught without them. In these units, however, students' experience is greatly enhanced by computer use.

The following list outlines the recommended use of computers in this curriculum:

Kindergarten
Unit: *Making Shapes and Building Blocks* (Exploring Geometry)
Software: *Shapes*
Source: provided with the unit

Grade 1
Unit: *Survey Questions and Secret Rules* (Collecting and Sorting Data)
Software: *Tabletop, Jr.*
Source: Broderbund

Unit: *Quilt Squares and Block Towns* (2-D and 3-D Geometry)
Software: *Shapes*
Source: provided with the unit

Grade 2
Unit: *Mathematical Thinking at Grade 2* (Introduction)
Software: *Shapes*
Source: provided with the unit

Unit: *Shapes, Halves, and Symmetry* (Geometry and Fractions)
Software: *Shapes*
Source: provided with the unit

Unit: *How Long? How Far?* (Measuring)
Software: *Geo-Logo*
Source: provided with the unit

Grade 3
Unit: *Flips, Turns, and Area* (2-D Geometry)
Software: *Tumbling Tetrominoes*
Source: provided with the unit

Unit: *Turtle Paths* (2-D Geometry)
Software: *Geo-Logo*
Source: provided with the unit

Grade 4
Unit: *Sunken Ships and Grid Patterns* (2-D Geometry)
Software: *Geo-Logo*
Source: provided with the unit

Grade 5
Unit: *Picturing Polygons* (2-D Geometry)
Software: *Geo-Logo*
Source: provided with the unit

Unit: *Patterns of Change* (Tables and Graphs)
Software: *Trips*
Source: provided with the unit

Unit: *Data: Kids, Cats, and Ads* (Statistics)
Software: *Tabletop, Sr.*
Source: Broderbund

The software provided with the *Investigations* units uses the power of the computer to help students explore mathematical ideas and relationships that cannot be explored in the same way with physical materials. With the *Shapes* (grades 1–2) and *Tumbling Tetrominoes* (grade 3) software, students explore symmetry, pattern, rotation and reflection, area, and characteristics of 2-D shapes. With the *Geo-Logo* software (grades 2–5), students investigate rotations and reflections, coordinate geometry, the properties of 2-D shapes, and angles. The *Trips* software (grade 5) is a mathematical exploration of motion in which students run experiments and interpret data presented in graphs and tables.

We suggest that students work in pairs on the computer; this not only maximizes computer resources but also encourages students to consult, monitor, and teach each other. Generally, more than two students at one computer find it difficult to share. Managing access to computers is an issue for every classroom. The curriculum gives you explicit support for setting up a system. The units are structured on the assumption that you have enough computers for half your students to work on the machines in pairs at one time. If you do not have access to that many computers, suggestions are made for structuring class time to use the unit with fewer than five.

Assessment plays a critical role in teaching and learning, and it is an integral part of the *Investigations* curriculum. For a teacher using these units, assessment is an ongoing process. You observe students' discussions and explanations of their strategies on a daily basis and examine their work as it evolves. While students are busy recording and representing their work, working on projects, sharing with partners, and playing mathematical games, you have many opportunities to observe their mathematical thinking. What you learn through observation guides your decisions about how to proceed. In any of the units, you will repeatedly consider questions like these:

■ Do students come up with their own strategies for solving problems, or do they expect others to tell them what to do? What do their strategies reveal about their mathematical understanding?

■ Do students understand that there are different strategies for solving problems? Do they articulate their strategies and try to understand other students' strategies?

■ How effectively do students use materials as tools to help with their mathematical work?

■ Do students have effective ideas for keeping track of and recording their work? Do keeping track of and recording their work seem difficult for them?

You will need to develop a comfortable and efficient system for recording and keeping track of your observations. Some teachers keep a clipboard handy and jot notes on a class list or on adhesive labels that are later transferred to student files. Others keep loose-leaf notebooks with a page for each student and make weekly notes about what they have observed in class.

Assessment Tools in the Unit

With the activities in each unit, you will find questions to guide your thinking while observing the students at work. You will also find two built-in assessment tools: Teacher Checkpoints and embedded Assessment activities.

Teacher Checkpoints The designated Teacher Checkpoints in each unit offer a time to "check in" with individual students, watch them at work, and ask questions that illuminate how they are thinking.

At first it may be hard to know what to look for, hard to know what kinds of questions to ask. Students may be reluctant to talk; they may not be accustomed to having the teacher ask them about their work, or they may not know how to explain their thinking. Two important ingredients of this process are asking students open-ended questions about their work and showing genuine interest in how they are approaching the task. When students see that you are interested in their thinking and are counting on them to come up with their own ways of solving problems, they may surprise you with the depth of their understanding.

Teacher Checkpoints also give you the chance to pause in the teaching sequence and reflect on how your class is doing overall. Think about whether you need to adjust your pacing: Are most students fluent with strategies for solving a particular kind of problem? Are they just starting to formulate good strategies? Or are they still struggling with how to start? Depending on what you see as the students work, you may want to spend more time on similar problems, change some of the problems to use smaller numbers, move quickly to more challenging material, modify subsequent activities for some students, work on particular ideas with a small group, or pair students who have good strategies with those who are having more difficulty.

Embedded Assessment Activities Assessment activities embedded in each unit will help you examine specific pieces of student work, figure out what they mean, and provide feedback. From the students' point of view, these assessment activities are no different from any others. Each is a learning experience in and of itself, as well as an opportunity for you to gather evidence about students' mathematical understanding.

The embedded assessment activities sometimes involve writing and reflecting; at other times, a discussion or brief interaction between student and teacher; and in still other instances, the creation and explanation of a product. In most cases, the assessments require that students *show* what they did, *write* or *talk* about it, or do both. Having to explain how they worked through a problem helps students be more focused and clear in their mathematical thinking. It also helps them realize that doing mathematics is a process that may involve tentative starts, revising one's approach, taking different paths, and working through ideas.

Teachers often find the hardest part of assessment to be interpreting their students' work. We provide guidelines to help with that interpretation. If you have used a process approach to teaching writing, the assessment in *Investigations* will seem familiar. For many of the assessment activities, a Teacher Note provides examples of student work and a commentary on what it indicates about student thinking.

Documentation of Student Growth

To form an overall picture of mathematical progress, it is important to document each student's work. Many teachers have students keep their work in folders, notebooks, or journals, and some like to have students summarize their learning in journals at the end of each unit. It's important to document students' progress, and we recommend that you keep a portfolio of selected work for each student, unit by unit, for the entire year. The final activity in each *Investigations* unit, called Choosing Student Work to Save, helps you and the students select representative samples for a record of their work.

This kind of regular documentation helps you synthesize information about each student as a mathematical learner. From different pieces of evidence, you can put together the big picture. This synthesis will be invaluable in thinking about where to go next with a particular child, deciding where more work is needed, or explaining to parents (or other teachers) how a child is doing.

If you use portfolios, you need to collect a good balance of work, yet avoid being swamped with an overwhelming amount of paper. Following are some tips for effective portfolios:

- Collect a representative sample of work, including some pieces that students themselves select for inclusion in the portfolio. There should be just a few pieces for each unit, showing different kinds of work—some assignments that involve writing as well as some that do not.

- If students do not date their work, do so yourself so that you can reconstruct the order in which pieces were done.

- Include your reflections on the work. When you are looking back over the whole year, such comments are reminders of what seemed especially interesting about a particular piece; they can also be helpful to other teachers and to parents. Older students should be encouraged to write their own reflections about their work.

Assessment Overview

There are two places to turn for a preview of the assessment opportunities in each *Investigations* unit. The Assessment Resources column in the unit Overview Chart identifies the Teacher Checkpoints and Assessment activities embedded in each investigation, guidelines for observing the students that appear within classroom activities, and any Teacher Notes and Dialogue Boxes that explain what to look for and what types of student responses you might expect to see in your classroom. Additionally, the section About the Assessment in This Unit gives you a detailed list of questions for each investigation, keyed to the mathematical emphases, to help you observe student growth.

Depending on your situation, you may want to provide additional assessment opportunities. Most of the investigations lend themselves to more frequent assessment, simply by having students do more writing and recording while they are working.

Timelines and Rhythm Patterns

Content of This Unit   During this 2-week unit, students explore concepts of time and rhythm patterns. Sequencing actions or events in time is one mathematical idea that extends throughout the unit. In both investigations, students communicate actions or events in time through visual representations.

During the first investigation, students explore a variety of timeline representations. They assemble a timeline that has been provided, then create timelines of important events in their lives. They also create 24-hour timelines of events that make a day "special." They compare lengths of time it takes to do "special activities" through a guessing game and a performance.

In the second investigation, students explore mathematical patterns expressed in rhythms. They invent and develop ways of representing and interpreting them. They use body actions (such as clapping) to act out rhythms and record their rhythms on paper. The class develops a shared code in which a particular symbol stands for an action. Students establish conventions for communicating rhythms, then look at traditional musical notation and compose their own two-part rhythm music.

Connections with Other Units   If you are doing the full-year *Investigations* curriculum in the suggested sequence for grade 2, this is the last of eight units. If you have done the grade 2 data units *(Does It Walk, Crawl, or Swim?* and *How Many Pockets? How Many Teeth?),* students will be familiar with the idea of inventing their own representations. Working with the routine Time and Time Again this year will also support students' work in this unit.

This unit lays the foundation for ideas that students will reencounter and extend in the "Mathematics of Change" strand that extends through the grade levels of the *Investigations* curriculum (*Up and Down the Number Line* in grade 3, *Changes Over Time* in grade 4, and *Patterns of Change* in grade 5). This unit can be successfully used at grade 3, depending on the previous experience and needs of your students.

Investigations Curriculum ■ Suggested Grade 2 Sequence

Mathematical Thinking at Grade 2 (Introduction)

Coins, Coupons, and Combinations (The Number System)

Does It Walk, Crawl, or Swim? (Sorting and Classifying Data)

Shapes, Halves, and Symmetry (Geometry and Fractions)

Putting Together and Taking Apart (Addition and Subtraction)

How Long? How Far? (Measuring)

How Many Pockets? How Many Teeth? (Collecting and Representing Data)

▶ *Timelines and Rhythm Patterns* (Representing Time)

Investigation 1 ▪ Timelines

Class Sessions	Activities	Pacing
Sessions 1 and 2 (p. 4) WHAT IS A TIMELINE?	What Is a Timeline? Creating a Dr. Seuss Timeline Introducing Math Folders and Weekly Logs Homework: Life Timelines Extension: Displaying the Timeline Extension: Reading Time	minimum 1 hr
Session 3 (p. 14) TIMELINE OF MY LIFE	Planning Your Timeline A Timeline of My Life Homework: Special Day Activities Extension: Timeline of the Future	minimum 1 hr
Sessions 4 and 5 (p. 20) SPECIAL DAY TIMELINES	Brainstorming Special Activities A Class Timeline Special Day Timelines Secret Timelines Homework: Events in an Adult's Life Extension: Reading Children's Literature	minimum 2 hr
Session 6 (p. 31) ACTING OUT TIMELINES	Teacher Checkpoint: Counting on Timelines Acting Out Timelines Homework: Special Day Stories Extension: Timeline Display Extension: Timing Devices	minimum 1 hr
Start-Up ▪ Today's Number, Time and Time Again		

Mathematical Emphasis

- Sequencing events
- Representing events in time
- Comparing durations of time within a day
- Developing familiarity with time notation

Assessment Resources

Marking Events in Time (Teacher Note, p. 11)

Keeping Track of Students' Work (Teacher Note, p. 12)

For How Many Years . . . ? (Dialogue Box, p. 13)

A Timeline of My Life: Observing the Students (p. 17)

Timelines of Our Lives (Dialogue Box, p. 19)

Special Day Timelines: Observing the Students (p. 25)

Duration (Teacher Note, p. 28)

Showing How Long (Dialogue Box, p. 30)

Teacher Checkpoint: Counting on Timelines (p. 31)

Materials

Student math folders

Miss Rumphius by Barbara Cooney (opt.)

Counters

100 chart

Chart paper

Adding machine tape

Crayons or markers

Scissors

Timer

Analog clock

Digital clock

Paste or glue stick

Family letter

Student Sheets 1–8

Teaching resource sheets

Investigation 2 ■ Rhythm Patterns

Class Sessions	Activities	Pacing
Session 1 (p. 36) FOLLOW-THE-LEADER RHYTHM GAME	Follow-the-Leader Rhythm Game Introducing Rhythm Representations Interpreting Rhythm Representations Homework: Follow-the-Leader Rhythm Game	minimum 1 hr
Sessions 2 and 3 (p. 46) CODES AND CONVENTIONS	More Rhythm Sharing Agreeing on Three Symbols Assessment: Guess My Rhythm Class Discussion: Establishing Conventions More Guess My Rhythm Homework: Guess My Rhythm Extension: Follow-the-Leader Rhythm Game	minimum 2 hr
Session 4 (p. 56) GUESS MY 3 RHYTHMS	Guess My Three Rhythms More Guess My Three Rhythms Homework: Things That Have to Do with Time	minimum 1 hr
Session 5 (p. 59) TIMING AND RHYTHMS	Rhythms in Music: "Bingo" Composing Rhythm Music Choosing Student Work to Save	minimum 1 hr

Start-Up ■ Today's Number, Time and Time Again

Mathematical Emphasis

- Inventing rhythm patterns using body actions

- Representing rhythm patterns showing sequencing and time

- Communicating with and interpreting written symbols and codes

Assessment Resources

Observing the Students (p. 39)

Representing Rhythm Patterns (Teacher Note, p. 41)

Investigating Rhythm Patterns (Dialogue Box, p. 43)

Interpreting Rhythm Patterns (Dialogue Box, p. 44)

Assessment: Guess My Rhythm (p. 48)

Observing the Students (p. 52)

Establishing Conventions (Teacher Note, p. 54)

Codes, Conventions, and Pauses (Dialogue Box, p. 55)

Observing the Students (p. 58)

Observing the Students (p. 62)

Choosing Student Work to Save (p. 63)

Materials

Max Found Two Sticks by Brian J. Pinkney (opt.)

Paper, 8 1/2" × 11"

Construction paper

Chart paper

Markers or crayons in dark colors

Timer

Analog clock

Digital clock

Tape or glue

Student Sheets 9–12

Following are the basic materials needed for the activities in this unit. Many of the items can be purchased from the publisher, either individually or in the Teacher Resource Package and the Student Materials Kit for grade 2. Detailed information is available on the *Investigations* order form. To obtain this form, call toll-free 1-800-872-1100 and ask for a Dale Seymour customer service representative.

Student math folders

Chart paper

Counters (such as buttons, a number line, a 100 chart)

Snap™ Cubes (interlocking cubes): 1000

Adding machine tape: 3–4 rolls

Paste or glue sticks: 1 per student

Markers or crayons

Tape

Letter-size paper: about 200 sheets

Construction paper: about 30 sheets

Timer (optional)

Analog clock (optional)

Digital clock (optional)

Miss Rumphius by Barbara Cooney (optional)

Max Found Two Sticks by Brian J. Pinkney (optional)

The following materials are provided at the end of this unit as blackline masters. A Student Activity Booklet containing all student sheets and teaching resources needed for individual work is available.

Family Letter (p. 76)

Student Sheets 1–12 (p. 77)

Teaching Resource:

    Dr. Seuss Timeline (p. 85)

Practice Pages (p. 95)

Related Children's Literature

Aardema, Verna. *Why Mosquitoes Buzz in People's Ears*. New York: Dial, 1975.

Adler, David A. *Picture Book Biographies*. New York: Holiday House, 1989–1995.

Cooney, Barbara. *Miss Rumphius*. New York: Viking, 1982.

Hutchins, Pat. *Clocks and More Clocks*. New York: Macmillan, 1970.

Levinson, Riki. *Country Dawn to Dusk*. New York: Dutton Children's Books, 1992.

Lewis, Paul Owen. *P. Bear's New Year's Party.* Hillsboro, Ore.: Beyond Words Publishing, 1989.

Pinkney, Brian J. *Max Found Two Sticks*. New York: Simon and Schuster, 1994.

Pluckrose, Henry. *Math Counts: Time*. Chicago: Children's Press, 1995.

Waddell, Martin. *The Happy Hedgehog Band*. Cambridge, Mass.: Candlewick Press, 1991.

Watts, Barrie. *See How They Grow* series. New York: Dutton, 1991.

Williams, Vera B. *Three Days on a River in a Red Canoe*. New York: Greenwillow Books, 1981.

Zolotow, Charlotte. *This Quiet Lady.* New York: Greenwillow Books, 1992.

This unit is about time and ways to represent actions or events that happen over time. Time is a complex experience that is a part of students' lives from birth. It is useful to distinguish among three aspects in the way we think of time: sequence, duration, and cycles.

Sequence The notion of sequence is essential to an understanding of time. *Before*, *during*, and *after* are words that arise whenever time is an issue. More often than not, we use irregular time scales. For example, someone might describe some of the activities during a day in this way: "After breakfast, I go to work. When I come home, dinner is ready." This statement describes a sequence of three phases: breakfast, work, dinner. No indication is given that breakfast may have taken 20 minutes and work 7 hours; only the sequential order is described. This is the approach that children often use when they are asked to represent their activities over a day. Children tend to draw an ordered sequence (go to school, play at home, watch television) in which the relative duration of each activity is not represented.

In this unit, students create and represent sequences of events. Some events, such as important moments in a lifetime or special activities in a day, are marked along a timeline divided evenly into years or hours. Body actions producing the sounds of a rhythm are represented without the constraint of a regular scale. All of these events are ordered according to their sequence in time.

Duration Everyone can agree that some things take too long and others end too soon. Our perception of duration is greatly influenced by events in which we are involved. For example, a child who had great fun with friends during an afternoon might be surprised at the "sudden" fact that it is time to go home, whereas her brother, who was ill, could feel that the same afternoon lasted an eternity. They may both know that the afternoon lasted the same number of hours, but their inner perceptions of duration may convey their sense of time more meaningfully than their reading of the clock. As children become more familiar with concepts of time, they may develop good ideas of duration for some activities (for example, how long it takes to walk home from school) but have only vague ideas about others (for example, time spent sleeping).

By creating timelines in which length on paper indicates duration of time spent doing an activity, students learn to quantify duration and compare activities against the background of a *regular* time scale. Activities that take more time are displayed with a longer segment. These segments are punctuated by instances that mark the beginning or the end of an activity. A continuous timeline helps to raise questions about the "in between" times that children often ignore when they focus purely on a sequence of events.

Cycles One aspect of measuring time is keeping track of cycles. Repeating years, days, and hours are common cycles that students will encounter in their work in the first investigation, Timelines. The recurrent turn of a clock's hands is a way of keeping track of the time of day. Describing what happens within one cycle (for example, winter follows fall, spring follows winter) often suffices to tell what will always happen. Noon on one day starts a pattern of time that is repeated starting at noon the next day. Birthdays, regular daily activities, and school years are all recurring events that children use to make sense of the flow of time.

The second investigation, Rhythm Patterns, also engages students in thinking about cycles of time. Just as students explore patterns through connecting colored cubes, students in this investigation explore a sequence of actions (with sound) that is repeated. Students represent rhythms by inventing a code and decide how to show on paper that rhythm patterns continue to repeat in a regular way.

At the beginning of each investigation, the Mathematical Emphasis section tells you what is most important for students to learn about during that investigation. Many of these understandings and processes are difficult and complex. Students gradually learn more and more about each idea over many years of schooling. Individual students will begin and end the unit with different levels of knowledge and skill, but all will gain greater knowledge about rhythm patterns, time, and ways of representing them.

Throughout the *Investigations* curriculum, there are many opportunities for ongoing daily assessment as you observe, listen to, and interact with students at work. In this unit, you will find this Teacher Checkpoint:

Investigation 1, Session 6:
Counting on Timelines (p. 31)

This unit also has this embedded assessment activity:

Investigation 2, Sessions 2–3:
Guess My Rhythm (p. 48)

In addition, you can use almost any activity in this unit to assess your students' needs and strengths. Listed below are questions to help you focus your observation in each investigation. You may want to keep track of your observations for each student to help you plan your curriculum and monitor students' growth. Suggestions for documenting student growth can be found in the section About Assessment.

Investigation 1: Timelines

■ How do children sequence events or put them in order? How familiar are they with the language used when sequencing events, such as *before, after, during, between?*

■ How do children represent events in time? How are they deciding where events belong on their timelines? Do they show any understanding of the interval between markings? For example, how do they figure out where to put events that happened just before they turned one or when they were three and a half? Can you tell the order of events by looking at the timeline?

■ Are children able to use timelines to compare amounts of time? For example, how do they compare the time spent doing one activity (such as swimming) to the amount of time spent doing a different activity (such as playing the piano)?

■ How familiar are students with time notation such as, 3:00, three o'clock, A.M., and P.M.?

Investigation 2: Rhythm Patterns

■ Are students able to invent and/or follow rhythm patterns using body actions? Do they recognize these rhythms as patterns that repeat? Can they identify the part that repeats?

■ How do students represent rhythm patterns? Are students able to use symbols to record a rhythm? Do their sequences of symbols correspond to the rhythms they create? How? Do they include pauses? How? Do they indicate longer or shorter intervals between actions? How?

■ Do students see the representation of rhythm patterns as a means of communication? Or do they view it as an opportunity to "stump" everyone? Do they adjust their representations when others interpret the rhythm pattern differently than was intended? How? Are students able to interpret others' rhythm patterns? Are they able to offer suggestions that help clarify others' rhythm patterns?

In the *Investigations* curriculum, mathematical vocabulary is introduced naturally during the activities. We don't ask students to learn definitions of new terms; rather, they come to understand such words as *factor* or *area* or *symmetry* by hearing them used frequently in discussion as they investigate new concepts. This approach is compatible with current theories of second-language acquisition, which emphasize the use of new vocabulary in meaningful contexts while students are actively involved with objects, pictures, and physical movement.

Listed below are some key words used in this unit that will not be new to most English speakers at this age level but may be unfamiliar to students with limited English proficiency. You will want to spend additional time working on these words with your students who are learning English. If your students are working with a second-language teacher, you might enlist your colleague's aid in familiarizing students with these words before and during this unit. In the classroom, look for opportunities for students to hear and use these words. Activities you can use to present the words are given in the appendix, Vocabulary Support for Second-Language Learners (p. 73).

born, birthday, older, younger Students create timelines of their lives, indicating significant activities that occurred from the time they were born until the present time.

morning, afternoon, evening, breakfast, lunch, dinner, activities Students create Special Day Timelines which include special activities they like to do. Students use morning, afternoon, evening, or breakfast, lunch, dinner as benchmarks for their timelines.

Multicultural Extensions for All Students

Whenever possible, encourage students to share words, objects, customs, or any aspects of daily life from their own cultures and backgrounds that are relevant to the activities in this unit. For example:

■ In Investigation 1, as students assemble their timelines, they may enjoy sharing words for ages and times they know in other languages. Encourage students to teach these terms to others in the class.

■ When students finish discussing important events in the life of Dr. Seuss during Investigation 1, you might invite them to contribute any information they have about authors who are famous in other countries, including those in which English is not the primary language.

■ As students are creating their Special Day Timelines in Investigation 1, discrepancies may arise as to what time of the day common events occur. For example, in some cultures supper is eaten at a much later time in the evening than in others. Discuss reasons for these differences, and make certain students understand that it is not necessary for everyone to do the same things at the same times during the day.

■ In Investigation 2, after students have finished singing the song "Bingo," invite them to share children's songs they know in languages other than English. The music teacher might be able to suggest some songs for students to sing. Or you may want to invite a family member in to teach the class a song in another language.

Investigations

INVESTIGATION 1

Timelines

What Happens

Sessions 1 and 2: What Is a Timeline? As a class, students assemble a timeline about the life of Dr. Seuss and discuss the important events in his life. For homework, students collect information about key events in their own lives.

Session 3: Timeline of My Life Students create timelines of their lives using information they collected for homework. They figure out where their significant life events belong and then compare their timelines. For homework, students plan a special day, deciding which activities they would like to do in the morning, afternoon, and evening.

Sessions 4 and 5: Special Day Timelines Students brainstorm activities for a special day. In pairs, they create a timeline of a special day and play a guessing game, Secret Timelines, figuring out where another pair's activities fit in a day.

Session 6: Acting Out Timelines In pairs, students compare the time it takes to do various activities within their own special days. Students act out their Special Day Time-lines by performing their daily activities on a time scale much shorter than a day.

Mathematical Emphasis

- Sequencing events
- Representing events in time
- Comparing durations of time within a day
- Developing familiarity with time notation

What to Plan Ahead of Time

Materials

- Student math folders (Sessions 1–2)
- *Miss Rumphius* by Barbara Cooney (Sessions 1–2, optional)
- Counters such as interlocking cubes, buttons, 100 chart (Sessions 1–2, optional)
- Chart paper (Sessions 1–2)
- Adding machine tape: 3–5 rolls (Sessions 1–2)

- Crayons or markers (Sessions 3–5)
- Scissors (Sessions 4–5)
- Timer (Sessions 4–5, optional)
- Analog clock (Sessions 4–5, optional)
- Digital clock (Sessions 4–5, optional)
- Paste or glue sticks (Sessions 4–5)

Continued on next page

What to Plan Ahead of Time (*continued*)

Other Preparation

■ Duplicate student sheets and teaching resources (located at the end of this unit) in the following quantities. If you have Student Activity Booklets, copy only the items marked with an asterisk, including any extra materials needed.

For Sessions 1–2

Family letter* (p. 76): 1 per student. Remember to sign and date the letter before copying it.

Student Sheet 1, Weekly Log (p. 77): 1 per student. At this time, you may wish to duplicate a supply to last for the entire unit and distribute the sheets as needed.

Dr. Seuss Timeline* (p. 85): 1 set for the class. Cut out the strips on each page.

Student Sheet 2, Life Timelines (p. 78): 1 per student (homework). If possible, send this sheet home with each student before you begin the unit so that students have two nights to complete the homework.

For Session 3

Student Sheet 3, Special Day Activities (p. 79): 1 per student (homework)

For Sessions 4–5

Student Sheets 4 and 5, Special Day Timeline (pp. 80–81): 2 of each per pair, plus extras* for display

Student Sheet 6, Events in an Adult's Life (p. 82): 1 per student (homework)

For Session 6

Student Sheet 7, Time Information About My Special Day (p. 83): 1 per pair

Student Sheet 8, Special Day Stories (p. 84): 1 per student (homework)

■ Prepare a math folder for each student if you did not do so for a previous unit. (Sessions 1–2)

■ *Miss Rumphius* by Barbara Cooney is used in this session. If that book is not available, select a biography to read aloud. (Sessions 1–2)

■ Prepare a sample timeline by folding a strip of 4-foot-long adding machine tape in half end to end, four times. Write BORN at the left edge and then write 1 at the first fold. Continue writing the years on the folds until you reach 8. See Planning Your Timeline (p. 14) for an illustration. (Session 3)

■ Cut apart adding machine tape into strips about 4' long. Cut 1 per student plus several extras. Students older than 8 can add a 6" section to their timeline for each additional year. (Session 3)

■ Prepare a sample of the Special Day Timeline by cutting apart the strips from a copy of Student Sheets 4 and 5 and gluing them together in order. Plan a place where you can display this timeline at a height within students' reach. (Sessions 4–5)

■ Arrange a space in your classroom that is large enough for five to six students to perform their Special Day Timelines at one time. (Session 6)

What Is a Timeline?

What Happens

As a class, students assemble a timeline about the life of Dr. Seuss and discuss the important events in his life. For homework, students collect information about key events in their own lives. Their work focuses on:

■ working within a regular scale
■ counting on a timeline

Start-Up

Today's Number   Today's Number is one of the routines that are built into the grade 2 *Investigations* curriculum. Routines provide students regular practice in important mathematical ideas such as number combinations, counting and estimating data, and concepts of time. For Today's Number, which is done daily (or most days), students write number sentences that equal the number of days they have been in school. The complete description of Today's Number (p. 64) offers some suggestions for establishing this routine and some variations.

If you are doing the full-year grade 2 *Investigations* curriculum, you will have already started a 200 chart and a counting strip during the unit *Mathematical Thinking at Grade 2*. Write the next number on the 200 chart and add the next number card to the counting strip. As a class, brainstorm ways to express the number.

If you are teaching an *Investigations* unit for the first time, here are a few options for incorporating Today's Number as a routine:

■ **Begin with 1**   Begin a counting strip that does not correspond to the school day number. Each day, add a number to the strip and use this number as Today's Number.
■ **Use the Calendar Date**   If today is the sixteenth day of the month, use 16 as Today's Number.

After Today's Number has been established, ask students to think about different ways to write the number. Post a piece of chart paper to record their suggestions. You might want to offer ideas to help students get started. If Today's Number is 45, you might suggest 40 + 5 or 20 + 25.

Ask students to think about other ways to make Today's Number. List their suggestions on chart paper. As students offer suggestions, ask the group if they agree with the statements. This gives students the opportunity to confirm an idea that they might have had or to respond to an incorrect suggestion.

Materials

■ Chart paper
■ *Miss Rumphius* (optional)
■ Counters (optional)
■ Student Sheet 1 (1 per student)
■ Dr. Seuss Timeline (1 set)
■ Student Sheet 2 (1 per student, homework)
■ Family letter (1 per student)
■ Student math folder (1 per student)

As students grow more accustomed to this routine, they will begin to see patterns in the combinations, have favorite kinds of number sentences, or use more complicated types of expressions. Today's Number can be recorded daily on the Weekly Log. (See p. 9.)

What Is a Timeline?

Introduce this investigation by reading *Miss Rumphius* by Barbara Cooney to students. *Miss Rumphius* is about the different stages in the life of a woman who tries to make the world more beautiful.

If this book is unavailable, read another book about someone's life. Select a biography about someone in whom your class is interested, or tell a biographical story that you know well. The *Picture Book Biographies* by David Adler (see p. I-15) are additional resources for this activity.

After reading *Miss Rumphius*, explain to students that this story uses words and pictures to relate the important events in her life. With students' help, list some of these events in the order of their occurrence on the board (from left to right in a long row). Tell students that this is a timeline of the events in Miss Rumphius's life. A timeline can include words and pictures but always shows time moving along.

Ask students if they have seen timelines before. You may need to provide an example (such as the Dr. Seuss Timeline). Perhaps they will recall having studied a famous person's life or reading a biography in which events were marked in time.

As students may discover when creating their own timelines, it is difficult to choose "important events" from a lifetime's worth of activities. The following are examples of some of the important events that could be listed if you are reading *Miss Rumphius*:

listening to her grand- father	growing up	working in a library	meeting the Bapa Raja	climbing mountains	living by the sea	being sick	planting lupines	advising little Alice

Point out to students that we can see the order of events in this timeline, but we cannot tell how long each event takes.

Creating a Dr. Seuss Timeline

Dr. Seuss is best known as a children's author for his rhyming books, his playfulness with words, and his colorful illustrations. From *And to Think That I Saw It on Mulberry Street* in 1937 to *Oh, the Places You'll Go!* in 1990, Dr. Seuss published 47 books full of nonsensical charm. His "Beginner Book" series (including *The Cat and the Hat*) revolutionized the way children learn to read. Dr. Seuss has said, "more than anyone else, my mother (who chanted to me at bedtime) is responsible for the rhythms in which I write." If your class has not read any Dr. Seuss books, get a few from the library and read them to students at some point during this unit.

Begin this activity with a discussion about Dr. Seuss. Ask students what they know about him. If someone suggests that he was an author, encourage students to name Dr. Seuss books with which they are familiar. Then explain to students that they will make a timeline to learn about the important events in Dr. Seuss's life. They will also make timelines of the important events in their own lives. See the **Teacher Note**, Marking Events in Time (p. 11), for information on the usefulness of timelines.

Give one section of the Dr. Seuss Timeline to each student. (This timeline was compiled from information in the books *Dr. Seuss From Then to Now,* organized by the San Diego Museum of Art [New York: Random House, 1986] and *Dr. Seuss and Mr. Geisel* by Judith and Neil Morgan [New York: Random House, 1995].) There are 22 sections, so if you have more than 22 students, you will need to give out sections to some pairs of students. Distribution could be an interesting number problem for students, since it is a real problem that can be approached in a variety of ways. For example, if you have 30 students, 14 could each get one section, and 16 could share the other 8 sections.

Each of you has a section of a timeline that tells some of the important events in Dr. Seuss's life and how old he was when each event happened. Read your section. Then we will arrange ourselves in time order from left to right, beginning with when Dr. Seuss was born.

Who has the section that tells when and where he was born? Stand over here at the beginning. If anyone else has a section showing when Dr. Seuss was 15 years old or younger, come up and arrange yourself in order.

Students continue coming up a few at a time, lining up in order from left to right. You might call up three sections at a time by asking for students who have years 27 or less, 39 or less, 51 or less, 63 or less, 75 or less, then all the rest of the years. Encourage students to look at one another's strips and work together to decide where everyone should stand. When students have lined up, check to see that the sections are in the correct order. Then staple the sections together, being careful to position the strips so that the vertical connecting lines match. This will ensure that all the years on the timeline are the same distance apart.

Hang up the timeline a few feet off the floor. Have students sit in front of the timeline and ask volunteers to read the events in the different sections. Encourage students to describe what they notice about the timeline and explain how it is arranged. Then ask questions students can answer by looking at the timeline.

How old was Dr. Seuss when *The Cat in the Hat, Green Eggs and Ham, The Lorax,* [*name other class favorites*] were published? Where would you look to find out how old he was when his first children's book was published? his last children's book? (He was 33 when *And to Think That I Saw It on Mulberry Street* was published and 86 when *Oh, the Places You'll Go!* was published.)

Next, you will work with a partner. Using the timeline to help you, figure out for how many years children's books by Dr. Seuss were being published.

Students may count on the timeline itself or look at the difference in the ages when his first and last books were published and use addition and/or subtraction to solve the problem. If you are doing the full-year *Investigations* curriculum, students will have had experience with subtraction situations in the unit *Putting Together and Taking Apart*. Some students solve such problems by subtracting a smaller number from a larger one, some by counting down, and others by counting up or adding up from the smaller to the larger number. See the **Dialogue Box,** For How Many Years . . . ? (p. 13), for examples of ways students solved this problem.

Students record their answers and how they solved the problem using words, numbers, and pictures. They may use available materials to count with, such as interlocking cubes or other manipulatives, the Dr. Seuss timeline, a number line, or a 100 chart.

When students have finished, encourage them to pose other problems about the durations of events in the life of Dr. Seuss. Record students' ideas on chart paper. Students should pose questions that begin with "For how many years. . . ?," such as, "For how many years did Dr. Seuss live in California? For how many years was he married to his first wife?" The question, "How many books did Dr. Seuss write?" is also interesting but is not a problem about duration.

Post the list of questions in the hallway with the accompanying timeline for other classes to read. (See the Extension on p. 10 at the end of this session.)

If there is time, help students find partners with whom to share their solutions to the "how many years?" problem. Or you might find another time during the day for students to share solutions as a class.

Introducing Math Folders and Weekly Logs

If you are doing the full-year *Investigations* curriculum, students will be familiar with math folders and Weekly Logs. If this curriculum is new to students, tell them about one way they will keep track of the math work they do.

Mathematicians show how they think about and solve problems by talking about their work, drawing pictures, building models, and explaining their work in writing so that they can share their ideas with other people. Your math folder will be a place to collect the writing and drawing that you do in math class.

Distribute math folders to students and have them label the folders with their names.

Your math folder is a place to keep track of what you do each day in math class. Sometimes there will be more than one activity to choose from, and at other times, like today, everyone in the class will do the same thing. Each day you will record what you did on this Weekly Log.

Distribute Student Sheet 1, Weekly Log, and ask students to write their names at the top of the page. Point out that there are spaces for each day of the weeks and ask them to write today's date on the line after the appropriate day. If you are doing the activity Today's Number, students can write the number in the box beside the date.

❖ **Tip for the Linguistically Diverse Classroom** Encourage students who are not writing comfortably in English to use drawings to record in their Weekly Logs. If students demonstrate some proficiency in writing, suggest that they record a few words with their drawings. Students can also record a sample problem representative of each day's work.

Ask students for suggestions about what to call today's activities. Activity titles should be short to encourage all students to record what they do each day. List their ideas on the board and have students choose one title to write in the space below the date. Students should put their solutions to the Dr. Seuss problem into their folders.

Weekly Logs can be stapled to the front of the folders (each new week on the top so that students can view prior logs by lifting up the sheets).

During the unit or throughout the year, you might use the math folders and Weekly Logs in a number of ways:

■ to keep track of what kinds of activities students choose to do and how frequently they choose them

■ to review with students, individually or as a group, the work they've accomplished

■ to share student work with families, either by sending folders home periodically for students to share with their families or during student/family/teacher conferences

For more information on students' work, see the **Teacher Note**, Keeping Track of Students' Work (p. 12).

Sessions 1 and 2 Follow-Up

 **Homework**

Life Timelines   Send home the family letter or *Investigations* at Home booklet. If you have not already done so, give Student Sheet 2, Life Timelines, to students so they can collect information about key events in their lives. Explain that they will use this information to create their own timelines in the next session. Detailed instructions can be found on Student Sheet 2.

❖ **Tip for the Linguistically Diverse Classroom**   Read each question on Student Sheet 2 aloud, drawing pictures on the chalkboard or using actions to be sure that the questions are understood. It may be useful for students with limited English proficiency to draw pictures over key words in each question to help them remember the question at home.

 **Extensions**

Displaying the Timeline   Hang the Dr. Seuss Timeline in the hallway. Post a list of questions or problems generated by students for other classes to think about when they look at the timeline.

Reading Time   Read a Dr. Seuss book aloud to students.

Marking Events in Time

Throughout *Timelines and Rhythm Patterns* students use lines or strips of paper marked from left to right to show sequences of events happening over time. These representations fuse time and space so that a length on paper corresponds to a duration of time. Learning to communicate and express time along marked lines is a major component of the unit.

There is a remarkable parallel between time and space. Three aspects of time experience correspond to experience of space: duration, sequence, and cycle. About the Mathematics in This Unit (p. I-16) provides some background on these notions.

Language is used in such a way that words can refer to both time and space, such as, "my house is *after* his" (space) or "let's talk *after* lunch" (time). Space, however, has a property that is absent in time; it is something you can touch. You can, for instance, point to a corner of the table and say "put it here." There is no such equivalent in time. You cannot point somewhere and say "wait until this time" unless you use a spatial representation of time such as a calendar. With a calendar, for example, you can see the cycle of the days of the week repeating as well as the sequence of events in time.

One of the important features of the Dr. Seuss timeline is that events are marked in even intervals. Every year is represented by about 2 inches. Although second graders are unlikely to create a regular scale in their own work, they can make sensible observations of events in time when the timeline provided uses space as an indicator.

Students can also make sense of the ways that events are sequenced in time. Knowing that one event (breakfast) should go to the left of an event that happens after it (lunch) is an indication that students find the timeline representation meaningful. Notice the ways that students describe events in time by paying particular attention to different tenses students use. For example, "This book was just before that one," or "He was married here," or "When he was 35, Dr. Seuss had not written a lot of books."

In the Dr. Seuss timeline and in the timelines students will create of their own lives in Session 3, students mark key events in time. There is less focus on the duration of time between events. In the timeline they work with in Sessions 4, 5, and 6, they will be asked to think more about the duration of activities as well as when certain activities begin and end. In all of the timelines in this unit, horizontal lines are used as spatial representations of time. Horizontal lines are a common way of showing the passage of time but are certainly not the only way. If you see examples of vertical, cyclical, or other ways in which time is represented, share these with students.

Throughout the *Investigations* curriculum there are numerous opportunities to observe students as they work. Teacher observations are an important part of ongoing assessment. Although individual observations are snapshots of a student's experience with a single activity, considered over time they can provide an informative and detailed picture of a student. These observations can be useful in documenting and assessing a student's growth. They offer important sources of information when preparing for family conferences or writing student reports.

Your observations of students will vary throughout the year. At times you may be interested in particular strategies that students are developing to solve problems. Or you may want to observe how students use or do not use materials to help them solve problems. At other times, you may be interested in noting the strategy that a student uses when playing a game. Class discussions also provide many opportunities to take note of students' ideas and thinking.

Keeping observation notes on a class of 28 students can become overwhelming and time-consuming.You will probably find it necessary to develop some sort of system to record and keep track of your observations of students. A few ideas and suggestions are offered here, but you will want to find a system that works for you.

A class list of names is a convenient way of jotting down observations of students. Since the space is limited, it is not possible to write lengthy notes; however, when kept over time, these short observations provide important information.

Stick-on address labels can be kept on clipboards around the room. Notes can be taken on individual students and then these labels can be peeled off and stuck into a file that you set up for each student.

Alternatively, jotting down brief notes at the end of each week may work well for you. Some teachers find that this is a useful way of reflecting on the class as a whole and on the curriculum and on individual students. Planning for the next weeks' activities often develops from these weekly reflections.

In addition to your own notes on students, all students will keep a folder of work. This work and the daily entries on the Weekly Logs can document a student's experience. Together they can help you keep track of the students in your classroom, assess their growth over time, and communicate this information to others. At the end of each unit, there is a list of suggestions of things you might choose to keep in students' folders.

For How Many Years...?

Dr. Seuss published his first book, *And to Think That I Saw It on Mulberry Street*, when he was 33 years old, and his last book, *Oh, the Places You'll Go!*, when he was 86. In this discussion during the activity Creating a Dr. Seuss Timeline (p. 6), students use that information to solve this problem posed by the teacher.

How can you use this timeline to figure out for how many years Dr. Seuss books were published?

[*Chen begins by walking up and down the timeline and finding the important events and ages in the problem. Then he returns to the spot where Dr. Seuss turned 33 years old and starts counting up, one by one, touching each year as he does so.*]

Ebony: No, not like that. Just count by 10's. And then take away 3 at the end. No, plus 3. [*Ebony counts by 10's, starting at 30 and ending at 80, and gets 50. She adds 6 to get to 86. This gives her the sum 56. Then she tries to figure out how to compensate for starting on 30 instead of 33.*]

Ebony: It couldn't be take away 3 because it would have had to be 27. At first I thought 40 something, but it's 59.

Chen, how were you thinking about this problem?

Chen: I counted till it was 20 years, right there, at 50 years old.

Ebony: No, that was 17 years.

Why do you think 17?

Ebony: Because he started writing at 33, not 30.

Chen: I kind of did it like I was counting by 10's.

Where did you start? How long was it right here [*at 33*]?

Chen: Zero. Oh, OK. Wait. [*He starts at 33 and counts every 10 years by 1's, touching each year.*] That's 10 years [*age 43*]. [*He continues with the same strategy.*] That's 20 [*age 53*].

So you think he'd been writing for 20 years when he was 53? Ebony, what did you find out?

Ebony: I took 33 and plussed 10 to 43 and plussed 10 again and it equaled 20 years, and then take away 3 is 17. So he'd been writing for 17 years then [*at age 50*]. So I agree with Chen. When he was 53, that was 20 years.

Carla, how did you figure out how many years altogether?

Carla: I put when he started and when he finished and the years in between. It was from 33 to 86. Then I thought, if I did 33 plus 7 it would get me to 40. Plus 10, 20, 30, 40. Plus 40 would get me to 80 years old. Plus 6 more for 86. So 6 plus 40 plus 7. 40 plus 6 is 46, and then 4 from the 7 is 50. There's 3 left from the 7, so 3 plus 50 is 53. I think his books were published for 53 years.

Ebony, what do you think about that?

Ebony [*thinks quietly for a moment*]: I thought it'd be easy. But I made a big mistake. You take away 3 [*from 33 to get to 30, where she began counting*]. I thought if I took it away I'd have to plus it.

How did you know to take it away and not add it like you did before? What made you realize you had to take it away *again*?

Ebony: Well, nobody had 59. Then I remembered Chen said 53, which is 3 down from 56. Now I see if I start counting at 30 then it makes the line for how much time bigger than it really is. So I have to minus it in the end.

These students used a variety of strategies to compare the numbers 33 and 86. Although some students would consider this a subtraction problem, these students counted up from the lower number. They counted by 10's, used landmark numbers, and were comfortable taking numbers apart and putting them back together. For them, the timeline itself was an important tool in conceptualizing and solving this problem.

Timeline of My Life

What Happens

Students create timelines of their lives using information they collected for homework. They figure out where their significant life events belong and then compare their timelines. For homework, students plan a special day, deciding which activities they would like to do in the morning, afternoon, and evening. Their work focuses on:

- working with a scale that has regular intervals
- representing significant life events along an axis of time
- marking discrete landmarks along the continuous axis of time

Materials

- Student Sheet 2 (completed homework)
- Prepared sample timeline
- Strips of adding machine tape (1 per student, plus extra tape)
- Crayons or markers
- Student Sheet 3 (1 per student, homework)

Start-Up

Today's Number

- **Calendar Date**   If you are using the calendar date for Today's Number, brainstorm with students ways to express the number. Suggest that students include subtraction as a way to express the number. Record their expressions on chart paper so that they can be saved each day.

- **Number of School Days**   If you are using the number of school days as Today's Number, and the number is over 100, encourage students to focus on ways to make 100 using multiples of 5 and 10. For example, if the number is 162, one solution is $50 + 25 + 25 + 25 + 10 + 10 + 10 + 5 + 2$. Add a card to the class counting strip and fill in another number on the blank 200 chart.

For complete details on this routine, see p. 64.

For complete details on this routine, see p. 64.

Activity

Planning Your Timeline

Students will need their list of important events that they completed for homework (Student Sheet 2). Invite a few students to share an interesting item from their lists with the class. Write each event on the chalkboard along with the student's name and age. This information will be used later in the activity.

Now you know about how old you were when you did certain things in your life. But it might be hard to see on your homework list which important event happened first, which happened next, and which happened most recently. In the last math class, you put together a timeline of the important events in Dr. Seuss's life. Today you are going to be making timelines so that you can easily see the order of the important events in your life.

Display the prepared timeline.

```
┌─┬──┬──┬──┬──┬──┬──┬──┬──┐ ┌──┐
│B│  │  │  │  │  │  │  │  │ │  │
│O│ 1│ 2│ 3│ 4│ 5│ 6│ 7│ 8│ │ 9│
│R│  │  │  │  │  │  │  │  │ │  │
│N│  │  │  │  │  │  │  │  │ │  │
└─┴──┴──┴──┴──┴──┴──┴──┴──┘ └──┘
```

You will each be using a timeline like this one. What do you notice about this timeline? What are some ways in which this is like the Dr. Seuss timeline?

Students may notice features such as how many numbers there are on the timeline, that it looks like a ruler, and that it is shorter than the Dr. Seuss timeline.

Where on this timeline would your first birthday go? How can you tell? Here is where you were born. So where is the whole year of time in between being born and having a first birthday?

Encourage students to come up and point out their answers on the timeline as they explain their ideas.

Where is the place that shows being a little bit older than 1? How about older than 3 but almost 4? What about 4½?

On the board around the timeline you may want to write phrases that describe age; for example, "between 1 and 2," "2½," "a little more than 2," or "almost 4." These clues can help students decide where things belong as they work on their own timelines. Then direct students' attention to the list of important events written on the chalkboard.

Can you find something on this list or on your own list that happened before someone's first birthday? Where would you put this event on the timeline?

Can you find something on this list or on your own list that happened when someone was between 1 and 2? 6 and 7? [*Name other listed ages.*]

As students comment and point to the timeline, write or draw their responses in the appropriate places. You could also fill in an event or two yourself, drawing attention to how you decided where an event belonged on the timeline.

What if there were a few things that happened to you before you were 1? For example, if you sat up, got your first tooth, and said your first word before you were 1, how could you show all those things?

When you make a timeline of your own life, you will have to decide where to put the important events. Think about how to show on your timeline how old you were by where you are writing or drawing your important events.

Encourage discussion about how students will plan their timelines.

A Timeline of My Life

Distribute a strip of adding machine tape to each student. Demonstrate how to fold the strips as you give the following directions.

You will each make your own timeline. Fold your strip in half end to end. How many equal sections are there? Fold it in half again. How many equal sections are there now? If you fold it one more time, how many sections will there be?

Your sections should be about this big [*hold up sample*]. A birthday is at each fold. If you are older than 8, you can get an extra strip and add another section for each year to your timeline.

Next, use a crayon or marker to write the years on the folds just like on the timeline I've made. Write BORN at the left edge and then write 1 at the first fold. You can use your homework list to fill in important events using pictures and words. Use a pencil to start with in case you need to make changes.

Students older than 8 may need help extending their adding machine tape Life Timeline. Help them fold another entire timeline and cut it into pieces (along the folds) that are each one year long and attach these as necessary.

Students work on their timelines by filling in some or all of their important life events. They may add other events as well, based on ideas they get from other students. Remind them that they do not need to fill in every bit of space, nor do they need to show everything that happened to them, just important events that help to tell the stories of their lives.

Some students may need help getting started if they have little information or if it is written in a form that does not make sense to them, such as 18 months. The most important thing for them to do is put their life events in order. It is not necessary that they be able to work with months or fractions at this point. You can support them by helping to make sense of (or change) any ages that are written in months to approximate years. For example, "1 year 9 months" becomes "almost 2," or "3¼" becomes "a little older than 3." Then students can focus on deciding where on their timeline a particular event belongs. If students were not able to collect any information, they can rely on their memories of special events. See the **Dialogue Box,** Timelines of Our Lives (p. 19), for an example of a classroom discussion on deciding where to place events on a timeline.

Observing the Students As students are working, notice how they make sense of their timelines.

■ How are they deciding where events belong?

■ Can you discern the relative order of their events by looking at the timeline? (For example, within a year, are events to the left earlier in time than those to the right?)

As students finish, ask partners to compare their timelines.

Put your timelines together like this [*show one directly underneath another*]. **Look carefully at them and discuss what you notice. You may want to read them from the beginning. Ask each other questions about what you don't understand. Tell your partner what you find interesting about the important events in his or her life. I am writing these directions on the chalkboard to help you remember what to do:**

1. Read your partner's timeline.

2. Ask about anything that seems unclear.

3. Compare the timelines. Are some of the same events on both timelines? Are they in similar places?

4. Make any changes and additions to your timeline that you think are necessary.

Post all of the timelines so that the class can look at them. You may want to keep these posted throughout the year so students can add other events as they arise or as they remember them.

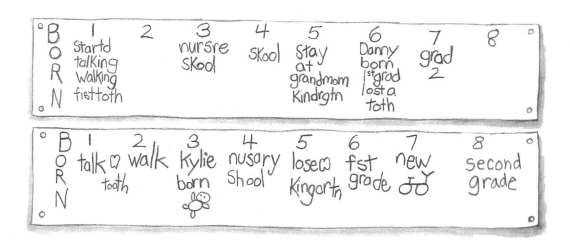

Session 3 Follow-Up

 **Homework**

Special Day Activities   Students imagine some of the activities they would like to do if they could invent a special day for themselves. Students make a list using the categories "morning activities," "afternoon activities," "evening activities," and "night activities" on Student Sheet 3, Special Day Activities. They will use some of this information in the next session.

❖ **Tip for the Linguistically Diverse Classroom**   As you list on the chalkboard the words *morning, afternoon,* and so on, draw a sketch above each word for students with limited English proficiency to copy. This may help them remember each word at home. Then suggest that students draw the activities they would plan for a special day.

Extension

Timeline of the Future   Students make timelines of the future by adding another strip of tape to their original timeline. With pictures and words, they tell the story of their hopes and plans for the next 8 years. Where do students hope to be in 2 years? in 5 years? What would they like to be doing? Students write stories that connect with their timeline of the future.

Timelines of Our Lives

In this discussion during the activity A Timeline of My Life (p. 16), the teacher asks students for their ideas on where they would place important events in their lives on a timeline.

Can anybody think of something that happened to you between 1 and 2, *while* you were 1 year old? Check your homework from last night.

Olga: I smiled.

So sometime after you were 1 and before you turned 2 you smiled. Do you know when?

Olga: I was 1 week old.

This question is hard, even for adults. Where would 1 *week* old be on the timeline?

[*Olga points to just past the 1-year-old mark. Graham points to just after the spot labeled BORN.*]

What do you think about these answers?

Simon: If it was over there, where Olga said, it would be 1 year and 1 week.

So Olga already had a whole year, her first birthday, and then 1 week later she smiled.

Simon: But, the other one that Graham pointed to, there's no birthday yet, so she's just 1 week old.

Where do you think you might put "starting school" on a timeline like this? Let's say this person started school when he was 4; he had 1 year of preschool.

Juanita: Some kids are born in August and some are born in other months. If the month goes by it might be different.

I agree it's a problem. What if all the information you had was that you were about 4?

[*Juanita points to just past the 4-year-old mark.*]

There will be decisions to make about where to place the events from your lives when they are not exactly on your birthday.

Juanita: So if you're 10, it [*timeline*] would go to 10. So write one important event for each year?

What if two really important events happened in one year? Suppose you got your first allowance at 5 and lost your first tooth at 5? How could you show those two things?

Helena: I would write them between 5 and 6. Maybe draw a line between the two things.

Salim: You could write one on top and one on the bottom. Or would you write what month?

Graham: I was thinking if one happened close to 5, I could write it near the 5. If the other one happened when I was almost 6, I could write it near the 6.

OK, so you'll have to make some decisions about that, too. I remember turning 8 and my dad saying to me, "You're starting your ninth year." I said, "No, I'm turning 8, it's my eighth year." But he was right, because I had finished 8 years. I couldn't believe it! When you turn 1, are you starting your first year?

[*Several students say that they would be starting their second year.*]

Students begin working. Some students struggle with how to place events that happened when they were less than 1 year old.

Trini: I started sitting up at 10 months. [*She starts at BORN and counts by 1's toward the 1-year mark, moving her finger a little farther to the right each time.*] Well, pretty far along here because there's only 12 months. [*She adds "sitting up" a little to the left of the 1-year mark.*]

Helena: Where's 6 months?

Trini: Halfway. Because 6 is half of 12.

Helena: So right in the middle of born and 1 year old.

Figuring out where to place events on a timeline with a regular scale (every year) is an important mathematical concept. Talking together as a class and then filling in their own timelines draws students' attention to the order of events from year to year as well as within a year.

Special Day Timelines

Materials

- Student Sheet 3 (completed homework)

- Prepared timeline (from Student Sheets 4 and 5)

- Student Sheets 4 and 5 (2 of each per pair)

- Crayons or markers

- Paste or glue sticks

- Scissors

- Analog clock (optional)

- Digital clock (optional)

- Timer (optional)

- Student Sheet 6 (1 per student, homework)

What Happens

Students brainstorm activities for a special day. In pairs, they create a time-line of a special day and play a guessing game, Secret Timelines, figuring out where another pair's activities fit in a day. Their work focuses on:

- sequencing events in time
- comparing durations of time within a day
- representing events in time

Start-Up

Today's Number

- **Calendar Date** If you are using the calendar date for Today's Number, brainstorm ways to express the number together with students. Suggest students include combinations of 10 as a way to express the number. For example, if the number students are working on is 23, and one number sentence is 10 + 10 + 3, ask them to find another way of making 10, such as 6 + 4 + 6 + 4 + 3. Record their expressions on chart paper.

- **Number of School Days** If you are using the number of school days as Today's Number, and the number is over 100, encourage students to focus on ways to make 100 using both addition and subtraction. For example, if the number is 163, possible solutions include: 200 − 100 + 63, or 50 + 50 + 70 − 7. Add a card to the class counting strip and fill in another number on the blank 200 chart.

For complete details on this routine, see p. 64.

Time and Time Again Time and Time Again is one of the classroom routines that are included in the grade 2 *Investigations* curriculum. This routine offers teachers ideas and suggestions for helping students develop an understanding of time-related ideas such as sequence of events, the passage of time, duration of time periods, and identifying important times in their day.

To use the version Timing 1 Hour, set a timer to go off at 1-hour intervals beginning on the hour. Choose a starting time and write down both the analog time (use a clockface) and the digital time. Every time the timer rings, record what time it is using analog and digital times. At the end of the day students make observations about the data collected. The complete description of Time and Time Again (p. 71) offers some suggestions for establishing this routine.

Brainstorming Special Activities

Students share some ideas from the special day they imagined for their homework. Explain that over the next few days students will create time-lines of a special day in their lives and will use them to play a guessing game, Secret Timelines. They will also act out their special day activities.

Tell students a story of what might be a special day for you, using mostly hour-long intervals and times that land on the hour. For example, "I like to sleep late, so on my special day, I'll get up at 11:00 A.M. and read in bed until 12 noon. Then I'll eat brunch. At 1:00 I'll exercise, and at 3:00 I'll shower and get dressed to go out. At 4:00 I'll meet a friend and walk around town. We'll have dinner at 6:00, and then we'll see a movie at 8:00. At 10:00 we'll go out for ice cream. I won't go to sleep until midnight."

You will create timelines for a special day. This special day will include activities that you would like to do. In order to make our Special Day Timelines, we will think about and agree on a list of six to eight special activities that you can choose from. We'll also have a list of required activities that you will need to include in your timeline.

Write the headings "Required Activities—use all" and "Special Activities—use some" on the chalkboard.

What are some activities that we do each day?

Including activities such as "waking up," "breakfast," "lunch," "dinner," and "going to sleep" will help structure the day. You may decide on differ-ent daily activities that better fit your students or use different names for these activities. List your choices under the "Required Activities" heading on the chalkboard.

❖ **Tips for the Linguistically Diverse Classroom** As you make the class list, decide with students on a simple picture to represent each idea. Sketch the picture beside each item on the list.

What activities would *you* want to have in your special day?

Ask students to use ideas from their homework to suggest special activities. List these under the "Special Activities" heading.

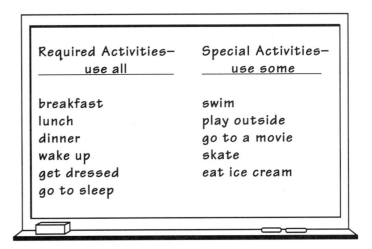

Required Activities—
use all

breakfast
lunch
dinner
wake up
get dressed
go to sleep

Special Activities—
use some

swim
play outside
go to a movie
skate
eat ice cream

Note: It may help if you list the special activities in a general manner. For example, if a student suggests play catch, you might write "play outside" and tell students they can choose to draw different outside activities. If students have ideas other than those listed, suggest ways to connect them with activities already on the lists.

What activities on these lists do you usually do in the morning? [*wake up, eat breakfast, get dressed*] **When might you go swimming or play outside?**

As you discuss the timing of activities, acknowledge that there are many possible times when they could be done.

Save these lists for use during following activities: A Class Timeline and Special Day Timelines.

Activity

A Class Timeline

Display the timeline you prepared from Student Sheets 4 and 5 by taping it to the chalkboard. Explain that first, as a class, students will create a Special Day Timeline, then partners will work to create their own Special Day Timelines. Begin by asking a volunteer to tell the time, then find it on the timeline. Note that for this timeline, only hours are used. See the **Teacher Note,** Time Notation (p. 29), for information on different ways to introduce students to timeline notation.

Where do you think morning hours are on this timeline? afternoon hours? evening hours? night hours?

On the board, write the headings "morning," "afternoon," "evening," and "night" above the approximate time spans on the timeline.

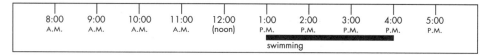

Decide with students which activities listed on the board everyone should include on their timelines when they make them. Then insert one or two of these activities on the class timeline. As you fill in each activity, ask students how long they think it would last and ask them to show that time span on the timeline. You may decide to add other activities to the timeline to give the day more structure. For example, all students might wake up at the same time and have breakfast at the same time. This may enable clearer comparisons later.

Add some special activities to the timeline and introduce a convention that shows the duration of each activity. A convention is a practice or a code that everyone in a group is aware of and agrees to use in order to facilitate a shared understanding.

I am going to show that swimming takes 3 hours by making a line from the time when the activity starts to the time when it ends. This line is one way to show how long the activity lasts.

8:00 A.M.	9:00 A.M.	10:00 A.M.	11:00 A.M.	12:00 (noon)	1:00 P.M.	2:00 P.M.	3:00 P.M.	4:00 P.M.	5:00 P.M.

swimming

Ask a volunteer to record "swimming" in the appropriate place on the timeline and to show how long the activity lasts by tracing a finger along the line.

What are some other ways we could show how long the activity lasts?

Students can also use pictures or repetitions of the word that describes the activity (for example, swim, swim, swim), but they need to use the line as well, since this is a convention that everyone will understand.

What if we have another activity that starts when swimming ends? How could we show that with a line?

Students may suggest using different color lines or using a symbol such as a vertical line or a dot in between the horizontal lines. Keep the class timeline hanging on the board so students can refer to it in the next activity, Special Day Timelines. Also save the lists of required and special activities.

Special Day Timelines

Students work with partners to create timelines. (Or you may want students to work individually.) They can refer to the completed class timeline on display for help getting started.

Distribute to each pair one set of Student Sheets 4 and 5, Special Day Timeline, and glue sticks and scissors so that students can put together their timelines. Students cut apart the strips along the dotted lines, then put glue on the gray areas and attach the strips. Remind them to look carefully at the times to be sure they are pasting their timeline in the correct order.

To complete your timeline, use all of the required activities listed on the board. You can also choose some special activities to add. Describe the activities in words or pictures. Mark where each activity begins and ends, and draw lines to show how long each activity lasts.

Note: What's important is that students become aware of the kinds of activities that occur in the morning, afternoon, evening, and night and that they develop a sense of time duration. If necessary, ask students to put the activities in an order that makes sense.

Encourage students to fill in all the space in their timeline. They can add other ways of showing time passing in addition to the horizontal line convention by including pictures in a sequence or by using different-colored lines to separate one activity from the next. Or students may express the duration of time using words (for example, "2 hours"). See the **Teacher Note**, Duration (p. 28), for more information on the duration of time. See the **Dialogue Box**, Showing How Long (p. 30), for examples of ways students determine how long activities last.

Observing the Students As students are working, notice what approaches they use to fill in their timelines. Some students may want to fill in their events in the order of the day (starting at 6 A.M. and going hour by hour), while others may want to fill in the required activities (breakfast, lunch, dinner, and sleeping) and then add the special activities.

- How are students making decisions about sequencing?
- How are they thinking about and showing the duration of time?
- Are their representations clear?
- How familiar are they with time notation?
- Do they seem to be developing a sense of time?
- Do they have a sense of what kinds of activities are done at different times of day and how long activities take?

Students work on their timelines until the end of Session 4 and through half of the next session. At the end of Session 4, you can store the unfinished timelines by hanging them vertically on a bulletin board facing inward. Since students will be playing a game called Secret Timelines, which involves guessing what is on another pair's timeline, they will need to work independently and not show their work.

Secret Timelines

During the last half of Session 5, students play the guessing game, Secret Timelines. All pairs need their completed timelines; new copies of Student Sheets 4 and 5, Special Day Timeline; glue sticks and scissors.

The goal of this game is to draw another pair's timeline activities on your blank timeline. But you cannot look at their timeline. You can ask any questions you want to, but you will have only 10 minutes. Try to get as much information as you can by asking questions. What are some questions you might ask to find out about someone else's day?

List students' suggested questions on the chalkboard. For example,

> What time do you start eating breakfast?
>
> Do you like to watch a lot of TV?
>
> How many different activities do you do?
>
> How long do you sleep?
>
> When do you eat lunch?

As you make the other team's timeline, write the activity names at the correct times. You do not need to draw pictures.

Ask students to find a pair whose Special Day Timeline they have not seen and sit across from them. One pair will have about 10 minutes to figure out what the other pair's day is like, then pairs will switch roles.

The partners who are guessing will try to fill in the empty timeline. The other partners should hold their Special Day Timeline so the guessers can't see it and should answer questions they ask but not offer any additional information.

Talk with your partner about what questions you will ask. When I say *start*, **begin asking questions and filling in the timeline, but don't let the other pair see what you're doing. When I say** *stop*, **you can compare both timelines to see how close you came to guessing the activities.**

❖ **Tip for the Linguistically Diverse Classroom** Pair second-language learners with other students who speak the same primary language. These partners can play the game in their native language.

Using an analog or digital clock or timer, time students so each pair has 10 minutes. When the first pair in each group has finished, have a brief discussion about what questions helped them get good information. Then students switch roles so that partners answering questions become guessers and original guessers answer questions. Students will need another 10 minutes.

As students are working, notice what kinds of questions they ask. Pay particular attention to those questions that lead to helpful information. Notice how students are answering the questions and how they are counting on their timeline.

When students have finished, discuss the results. Ask pairs to tell which activities were easy and hard to guess. If there is agreement about easy or hard activities, list these on the board under headings "Easy-to-Guess Activities" and "Hard-to-Guess Activities." Look at the lists together with students and discuss whether there are similarities in each list.

Look at the "Easy" list. Is there any way that these activities are alike? What about the activities on the "Hard" list?

What were some questions that gave you lots of information? What questions didn't give you much information at all?

List these on the board under the headings "Helpful Questions" and "Unhelpful Questions."

Why do you think some questions were helpful and others were not? Was it any easier to play the game the second time around?

Students will need to save these timelines to use in Session 6.

Sessions 4 and 5 Follow-Up

Events in an Adult's Life   Students talk with a parent or other adult in their household about important events in the adult's life. They record these events, using words or pictures on Student Sheet 6, Events in an Adult's Life.

 **Homework**

Reading Children's Literature   Read a book from the bibliography of Related Children's Literature (p. I-15), such as a book from the *See How They Grow* series. If these books are unavailable, read another book about growth or change over time.

 **Extension**

On their life timelines, students marked the years in which distinct events in their lives occurred. In the Special Day Timelines, they need to think about the duration of activities as well as when certain events begin and end. In working with timelines that have a regular scale (every hour), students use the idea that length indicates the duration of time. An activity that takes more time than another one is depicted with a longer segment. Students are asked to fill all the space in their Special Day Timelines and are introduced to the convention of using a horizontal line to communicate in a visual way how long it takes to do an activity.

Students will have other ideas about how to show how long an event lasts. Some students have used different-colored horizontal lines to distinguish among different activities and how long they take to do. Other students have colored the entire area that represents the hours they sleep.

Occasionally students have written the name of the activity many times (or in large letters) across an area (for example, 9 P.M. to 6 A.M. with "sleep, sleep, sleep" or "SLEEPING").

Students also use before and after pictures to punctuate the beginning, end, or other significant moments in an activity. Phoebe, for example, described "getting ready for riding" by showing a horse without a bridle over its head and, 1 hour later, a picture showing the bridle on the horse's head. See **Dialogue Box,** Showing How Long (p. 30), for more examples of ways students show the duration of time.

If students want to describe the duration of time using words (for example, "2 hours") on their timeline, this is fine. Encourage them also to show the duration of time in a visual way, which will make it easier for others to see whether an activity is long or short just by looking at it. As students are working, ask them how they are counting hours. Some of the issues that arise when students use number lines may arise here as well (for example, counting from 10 A.M. to 3 P.M. as 6 hours by counting 10, 11, 12, 1, 2, 3). The shared convention of the horizontal line will help students keep track of how many hours have gone by. Keep in mind that although students may understand that time never stops, the task of showing time passing is difficult even for adults.

Time Notation

Throughout the *Investigations* units, students encounter activities that deal with the mathematical aspects of time—sequence, duration, and cycles. They use years, months, or hours to show sequential events such as the Life Timelines, or changes that take place over time such as the growth of a plant; they solve problems about how many days need to pass before a special event, such as a class trip or a birthday; they figure out the duration of time between two events in hours or days. In the context of these investigations, students use time notation and read clocks and calendars. We do not spend time in this unit learning to read a clockface; rather, we use ideas about time within mathematical problem-solving situations.

If you are also helping students begin to "tell time," you can use this unit as a context for reading clockfaces and time notation. Most second graders are comfortable with the idea of hours and half hours, so you can begin with these familiar times. Consider working with times that are especially meaningful to your students, such as the times they get up, arrive at school, or have dinner. You can ask students questions about the school day such as, "What time does our class have lunch?" and post the time notation and a clockface on your school schedule.

In this unit, students are introduced to time notation in hours when they work on their Special Day Timelines that are marked in regularly spaced intervals of 1 hour. If you are interested in pursuing the teaching of time notation to your class, the activity Special Day Timelines offers a context in which to do this. For example, you might extend this activity by asking students what they have noticed about the way times are written on the Special Day Timeline. You could

ask students to write other times in the same fashion as the times on the chart, pointing out that the hour is written before the colon and that the minutes come afterward. Ask students what patterns they see in the numbers. You may also consider integrating time notation activities with those from the classroom routine Time and Time Again (p. 71). The activities in this routine complement the content of this unit.

During this investigation, students will be developing ideas about what times of day are indicated by A.M. and P.M. In addition to meaning morning and evening, you and your students may be interested in knowing that A.M. stands for ante meridiem (before noon) and P.M. for post meridiem (after noon). Also, you may want to mention that in Europe, Latin America, and U.S. military sites, a 24-hour clock is used. The 24 hours begin at midnight so that noon is 1200 hours (12 hundred hours) and the next hour is 1300 hours (13 hundred hours).

Showing How Long

8:00 get dressed	1:00 riding lessons	6:00 going home	10:00 go to bed

| 6 A.M. | 7 A.M. | 8 A.M. | 9 A.M. | 10 A.M. | 11 A.M. | 12 (noon) | 1 P.M. | 2 P.M. | 3 P.M. | 4 P.M. | 5 P.M. | 6 P.M. | 7 P.M. | 8 P.M. | 9 P.M. | 10 P.M. | 11 P.M. | 12 (midnight) | 1 A.M. | 2 A.M. | 3 A.M. | 4 A.M. | 5 A.M. |

Phoebe is working on her Special Day Timeline. In this discussion, which occurs during the activity A Class Timeline (p. 22), the teacher and a student (Paul) who is working on another timeline talk with Phoebe about what her timeline shows.

Phoebe: When I go to bed I think it's 10.

Paul: How long do you sleep for?

Phoebe: Until the next morning.

Is it 2 hours, 3 hours, 4 hours?

Phoebe [*counts on her fingers*]: 11, 12, 1, 2, 3, 4, 5. Actually, 7 hours, because I get up at 5. [*She adds a horizontal line to her timeline between 10 and 5 and a picture at each end.*]

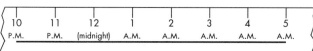

| 10 P.M. | 11 P.M. | 12 (midnight) | 1 A.M. | 2 A.M. | 3 A.M. | 4 A.M. | 5 A.M. |

So it seems like the next step for you is to think about what else happens during the day. I'm wondering what happens in between the riding lesson (1:00 P.M.) and going home (6:00 P.M.)?

Paul: I don't think driving home takes 5 hours. It doesn't take 5 hours to drive home unless you live in San Francisco [*from Cambridge, MA*].

What made you think about 5 hours, Paul?

Paul: Because of 1 and 6. Phoebe, how *long* is horseback riding?

Phoebe: 1 hour.

So if you start riding at 1 o'clock and do it for 1 hour, what time is it when you finish?

Phoebe: 2.

Is there a way you can show us how long you horseback ride, so that when we look at your timeline we can tell without asking you?

Phoebe adds "1 hour riding lesson" to her timeline and draws a horizontal line connecting 1:00 to 2:00.

And here it says you drive home at about 6:00, right? So what Paul and I are curious about is what you do in between your riding lesson and going home.

Phoebe: Maybe we can go out for dinner and then go home.

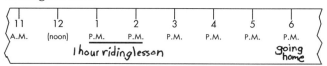

| 11 A.M. | 12 (noon) | 1 P.M. | 2 P.M. | 3 P.M. | 4 P.M. | 5 P.M. | 6 P.M. |

1 hour riding lesson   going home

In this conversation, Paul's questions get Phoebe thinking about the duration of time—in other words, how long various activities last. Phoebe figures out that she sleeps for 7 hours. She adds a horizontal line to show how long sleeping goes on and marks the important times (10 and 5) with pictures of sleeping and waking up.

For Paul, the blank space between 1 and 6 means that the activity "going home" lasts for 5 hours. Phoebe's solution to Paul's confusion is to use the horizontal line convention to show that riding lasts only 1 hour. Then she chooses other activities that fill the remaining time between 2 and 6. Filling in horizontal lines will help her to keep track of how long activities last.

Acting Out Timelines

What Happens

In pairs, students compare the time it takes to do various activities within their own special days. Students act out their Special Day Timelines by performing their daily activities on a time scale much shorter than a day. Their work focuses on:

■ enacting and observing events in time

■ experiencing a relative sense of time

■ comparing durations of time

Start-Up

Today's Number

Calendar Date *and* Number of School Days   Ask students to express Today's Number using multiples of 5 and 10. For example, if the number students are working on is 24 (calendar date), one solution is 20 + 5 − 1. If the number they are working on is 166, one solution is 25 + 25 + 25 + 25 + 20 + 20 + 20 + 5 + 1. If you are counting the number of school days, add a card to the class counting strip and fill in another number on the blank 200 chart. For complete details on this routine, see p. 64.

Materials

■ Student Sheet 7 (1 per pair)

■ Students' Special Day Timelines (from Sessions 4–5)

■ Prepared timeline (from Sessions 4–5)

■ Student Sheet 8 (1 per student, homework)

Activity

Teacher Checkpoint

Counting on Timelines

Give each pair of students Student Sheet 7, Time Information About My Special Day. They will also need their Special Day Timelines. The student sheet guides students to think about how long it takes to do each activity in their day.

Explain to students that they will answer the questions on this sheet, then practice acting out the activities in their Special Day Timelines without talking. Point out that the bottom of the sheet gives them a suggestion to help them keep track of time while they are performing. If students wish to make a prompt sheet, they can list their activities in order according to their starting times. Another way students can keep track of time as they are performing is for one student to point to the activities on the timeline while a partner acts them out. Each partner should have a chance to be the actor and the pointer if he or she wants to.

To help give students a sense of what they are rehearsing for, ask them to act out part of the class timeline (from Sessions 4 and 5) as a group. Post the class timeline on the chalkboard and use it to create a prompt sheet. Write starting times and activities in list form. For example:

6:00 A.M.	sleeping
7:00 A.M.	waking up and getting dressed
8:00 A.M.	breakfast
9:00 A.M.	baseball
11:00 A.M.	reading
12:00 noon	lunch

Begin a steady count (every 5–6 seconds or so) of the hours beginning at 6 A.M. For example, "6:00" (5 seconds later) "7:00." Students can act out these activities at their seats.

❖ **Tip for the Linguistically Diverse Classroom** Read each question on Student Sheet 7 aloud and use actions wherever possible to make the questions comprehensible for students. Or help students draw pictures over words that may be difficult for them to understand.

Use this activity and the student sheet to find out the different ways that students are counting on their timelines.

- How are students counting waking hours and sleeping hours?

- How are they making sense of this information given the fact that there are 24 hours in a day?

- How are they adding the waking and sleeping hours together?

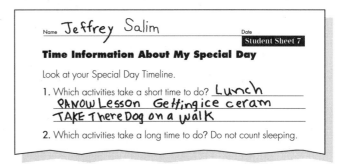

Name Jeffrey Salim

Date

Student Sheet 7

Time Information About My Special Day

Look at your Special Day Timeline.

1. Which activities take a short time to do? Lunch
PANOW Lesson Gettingice ceram
TAKE There Dog on a walk

2. Which activities take a long time to do? Do not count sleeping.

Activity

Acting Out Timelines

Arrange a space in your classroom large enough for five or six students to perform their special day activities while the remainder of the class observes. When students have had a few minutes to rehearse, organize them into groups to perform. Partners should be in the same group so that they can help each other when necessary. Provide several opportunities for students to perform, depending on your class size and how many students want to act out their timeline. It is not necessary for everyone to act out their timelines. The audience watches many different special days being performed at the same time.

One way to set up this activity is to have each performance take a few minutes. To help students, say the hour aloud, keeping to a steady rhythm (every 5–6 seconds), beginning at 6 A.M. Give students a general sense of the pace at which you will say the hours. You or a student may want to run a finger along a timeline so that other students (who are helping or performing) can see where you are.

After the first group performs their timelines, ask students what activities they could tell were being done just by watching.

What did you notice about those special day performances? Were any students doing the same things at the same times?

Give students who want to the opportunity to act out their timelines. After each group finishes performing, the students comment briefly on their experience performing or watching (what they liked, what they noticed).

Session 6 Follow-Up

Special Day Stories   Ask students to write stories about their special days on Student Sheet 8, Special Day Stories. In order for students to refer to their special day activities, have them fill out the top of Student Sheet 8 at school.

Homework

Timeline Display   Hang up students' timelines horizontally, one below the other (in the class or hallway). Post a list of questions nearby, as well as a blank piece of chart paper so that students may make written observations about each other's timelines. Questions might include:

Extensions

- Who got up earliest? What time was that?
- Who got up latest? What time was that?
- Who slept the longest? How long was that?
- Was anyone doing the same thing at the same time? Who? When?
- Who did the fewest activities in one day?

Timing Devices   If you and your students are interested in further exploring the passage of time, a timing device can be a visual source of support. *This Book Is About Time* by Marilyn Burns (Boston: Little, Brown and Company, 1978) and *Clocks, Building and Experimenting with Model Time Pieces* by Bernie Zubrowski (New York: William Morrow, 1988) offer explorations for students, including instructions for making simple timing devices.

Rhythm Patterns

What Happens

Session 1: Follow-the-Leader Rhythm Game As a whole class, students imitate a leader's rhythmic motions and discuss how they might represent them. Students represent a few rhythms in their own way and then interpret one another's rhythm representations as a class.

Sessions 2 and 3: Codes and Conventions Some students share their rhythm representations. The class chooses three symbols to represent three actions, and pairs of students use the symbols to make rhythm representations for each other to decode. Students discuss possible rules (conventions) for representing rhythms. Groups play a game called Guess My Rhythm.

Session 4: Guess My 3 Rhythms Students play a variation of Guess My Rhythm as a class and in small groups.

Session 5: Timing and Rhythms As a class, students look at traditional notation that shows how people represent time in music. In pairs they compose two-part rhythm music.

Mathematical Emphasis

■ Inventing rhythm patterns using body actions

■ Representing rhythm patterns showing sequencing and time

■ Communicating with and interpreting written symbols and codes

What to Plan Ahead of Time

Materials

- *Max Found Two Sticks* by Brian J. Pinkney (Session 1, optional)
- 8½"-by-11" paper for rhythm journals (see Other Preparation)
- Construction paper for rhythm journals (see Other Preparation)
- Chart paper (Sessions 1–3)
- Markers or crayons in dark colors (Sessions 1–5)
- Timer (Sessions 1, 4, 5, optional)
- Analog clock (Sessions 1, 4, 5, optional)
- Digital clock (Sessions 1, 4, 5, optional)
- Tape or glue (Session 4)

Other Preparation

- Duplicate student sheets and teaching resources (located at the end of this unit) in the following quantities. If you have Student Activity Booklets, no copying is needed.

For Session 1

Student Sheet 9, Follow-the-Leader Rhythm Game (p. 91): 1 per student (homework)

For Sessions 2–3

Student Sheet 10, Guess My Rhythm (p. 92): 1 per student (homework)

For Session 4

Student Sheet 11, Things That Have to Do with Time (p. 93): 1 per student (homework)

For Session 5

Student Sheet 12, "Bingo" (p. 94): 1 per student

- Prepare a rhythm journal for each student by folding in half five 8½"-by-11" sheets of paper and stapling them together to form a book. Use construction paper as a cover. Students can label the books *Rhythm Journal* and design their covers. (Session 1)

  Note: Students will continue to use their rhythm journals through Session 5.

- For homework, students are asked to bring from home items that have to do with time. These will be sorted and discussed during Session 5, Start-Up. (Session 4)

- Familiarize yourself with the song "Bingo" (Student Sheet 12) if you do not already know it. (Session 5)

Follow-the-Leader Rhythm Game

Materials

- *Max Found Two Sticks* by Brian J. Pinkney (optional)
- Chart paper
- Rhythm journals (1 per student)
- Markers or crayons
- Student Sheet 9 (1 per student, homework)

What Happens

As a whole class, students imitate a leader's rhythmic motions and discuss how they might represent them. Students represent a few rhythms in their own way and then interpret one another's rhythm representations as a class. Their work focuses on:

- inventing and repeating rhythmic patterns using body actions
- connecting written symbols with rhythmic actions
- creating visual representations to describe rhythms
- interpreting other students' rhythm representations

Start-Up

Today's Number

Calendar Date *and* Number of School Days Students express Today's Number using pennies, nickels, dimes, or quarters. For example, if Today's Number is 27 (calendar date), possible combinations include: 25¢ + 2¢ or 10¢ + 10¢ + 5¢ + 1¢ + 1¢. If Today's Number is 167, a possible combination is: 25¢ + 25¢ + 25¢ + 25¢ + 25¢ + 25¢ + 10¢ + 5¢ + 1¢ + 1¢. If you are keeping track of the number of school days, add a card to the class counting strip and fill in another number on the blank 200 chart.

Activity

Follow-the-Leader Rhythm Game

Ask students to sit in a circle so that they can all see one another. Introduce this investigation by reading the book *Max Found Two Sticks* by Brian J. Pinkney. This story is about a boy who finds two sticks and uses them to play rhythms that he hears and invents.

❖ **Tip for the Linguistically Diverse Classroom** Draw sketches on the board or have class members act out scenes to be sure the story is comprehensible to students with limited English proficiency.

As you read the book, students can tap on the floor or clap some of the rhythms that Max plays. If this book is not available, substitute another book about rhythms (such as *The Happy Hedgehog Band* by Martin Waddell, listed on page I-15), or spend some time discussing and trying rhythms using body motions.

We are starting a new investigation called Rhythm Patterns. You've probably noticed rhythm patterns in the world around you such as the beating of your heart and the beating of a drum. What are some other rhythm patterns you've noticed? What did they sound like?

Students may have ideas about rhythms they heard in music, while jumping rope or dancing, or while listening to such things as clocks ticking or animals running. They may also consider rhythms they can create with their bodies (such as clapping). Start a list of rhythms on chart paper. The list might include the name of the object and the sound it makes (horses galloping) or the sound itself (tap, tap, tap) as in *Max Found Two Sticks*. See the **Dialogue Box**, Interpreting Rhythm Patterns (p. 44) for examples of some observations second graders made about rhythms.

In this investigation we will be getting a feel for different rhythms by using our bodies to act them out. We'll also be thinking about how to show them on paper.

One thing mathematicians do when they are solving problems is to look for or invent regular repeating patterns. They also communicate patterns on paper using codes and graphs.

Introduce Follow-the-Leader Rhythm Game. Students may sit or stand to play, but sitting in a circle helps students focus on one another.

We're going to play a rhythm game. I'll be the first leader. I want you to follow along by copying my actions. [*Start a 2-beat rhythm, such as: Clap, slap thighs. Clap, slap thighs.*]

Now I'm going to try a different rhythm. Listen carefully and follow along.

Using the same actions, creating a 4-beat rhythm, such as: Clap, clap, slap thighs, pause. Clap, clap, slap thighs, pause.

What's the same about both of these rhythms? What's different?

Students may notice that the actions are the same, that the clapping is done twice (instead of once), or they may comment on the pause.

Who has another rhythm to show us? You can change the actions if you want to. [*Choose a student to be the leader.*] OK, watch what the leader does. Let's all do the same actions.

When students are mimicking the leader's actions together, invite the leader to call on someone else to change the rhythm. There will be a pause as the new leader begins the new rhythm.

Suggest that leaders use no more than five beats with no more than three different actions. Simple patterns allow students to focus on the rhythms.

If students are unsure about what kinds of actions to do or if their actions are inappropriate or difficult to imitate, you may want to stop the game and take a few minutes to brainstorm a list of possible actions. This is a good way for you to make clear to students what kinds of actions are acceptable in your class. Some actions other classes have used are: clapping, stamping, slapping thighs, tapping the ground, crossing hands on shoulders, tapping shoulders, tapping head, "swishing" (sliding) hands, snapping, and hitting elbows with hands.

Good actions for this game most often have both movement and sound. A visual gesture is continuous, but the inclusion of a sound provides a landmark in time. It is desirable for students to use actions that include both movement and sound during this investigation.

After a number of students have taken a turn being the leader, stop during a simple rhythm and begin the next activity by asking students to describe in words the rhythm they were just doing.

Activity

Introducing Rhythm Representations

What are some ways we could show the last rhythm we did without using words? Would someone come to the chalkboard and show us one way?

For example: "Clap, tap, stamp. Clap, tap, stamp" might be represented as:

+	x	•	+	x	•
(clap)	(tap)	(stamp)	(clap)	(tap)	(stamp)

Students may want to draw complicated pictures. Encourage them to use simple symbols and include how many of each action and the order of the actions.

Ask students to look carefully at the written representation and tell how it reflects the rhythm and the actions. Ask another student to represent the same rhythm in a different way.

After students have shared a few ideas for representing one rhythm, distribute a rhythm journal to each student. So that students can look back at their work, they will use rhythm journals throughout this investigation to record rhythm representations they create. Labeling the pages with dates will enable you to look at the progression of their work.

You'll use these rhythm journals to record all your rhythm patterns. For now, try showing two rhythms in your own way: the one we just did (clap, tap, stamp) and then a new rhythm that you make up. When you record your rhythm, think about a way of representing it without words so that another student could easily guess what the rhythm is.

As students begin, circulate to make sure they understand that their rhythm representation must be clear to others. Their ideas should be represented without using words. They may want to use dots or x's, letters or numbers, or even color codes and "map keys." Encourage students to use symbols they can repeat quickly to show the rhythm going through several cycles.

Allow enough time for students to record their ideas for both rhythms. If some students finish before others, they may choose a new rhythm to represent, or they may try and guess other students' rhythms from their representations.

Observing the Students As you watch students creating their rhythms, note what aspects of rhythm they communicate clearly. You can learn a lot about students' ideas of pattern, rhythm, communication, and organization by not providing too many rules for them to follow early in the process. Students can then discover the need for shared rules (conventions) for clear communication.

- Can you guess what rhythms students are depicting?
- Can students confirm whether your acting out of a representation is close to the right rhythm? If your guess isn't close, ask the student to explain the representation to you (in order to understand his or her thinking).
- Can students explain their rhythm representations to you and clarify the meaning of their drawings? (Talking through what they want to show often enables students to clarify their drawings.)

While you are observing students at work, select a few of the new rhythm representations that are clear and unique. Ask students to share their work at the end of this session and at the beginning of the next session. See the **Teacher Note**, Representing Rhythm Patterns (p. 41), for examples of how students represent rhythms.

Interpreting Rhythm Representations

Invite students whose rhythms you have selected to come up one at a time and record their rhythm patterns on the chalkboard or on chart paper. See the **Dialogue Box,** Interpreting Rhythm Patterns (p. 44), for an example of a classroom conversation about interpreting rhythms. Ask students what they notice about the rhythm patterns that are written on the chalkboard. Students take turns guessing what the creator of the rhythm was representing.

Encourage students to guess the rhythm by trying some actions that match the rhythm representation. If the guess is not what the creator intended, the creator may revise the representation (without talking) before the group guesses again. If it still is not clear, the creator explains what he or she meant, and the group discusses how the representation might be revised.

Emphasize to students that what's important is showing a rhythm so that a guesser can re-create it, not whether the guesser gets it "right." Then ask students to compare the rhythm representations.

Repeat the procedure of displaying rhythms and revising them as necessary with one or two other students. There will be time for more students to share their representations at the beginning of Session 2.

As this session ends, save the students' rhythm representations on the chalkboard or chart paper for reference during Session 2. Copy the additional representations that you have selected onto the chalkboard or chart paper for use at the beginning of Session 2.

You may want to remind students at some time during this investigation to record the work they have been doing in their Weekly Logs. Encourage them to share any problems they've been having or any interesting information they have found.

Session 1 Follow-Up

 **Homework**

Follow-the-Leader Rhythm Game   Students teach Follow-the-Leader Rhythm Game to someone at home and record one rhythm on Student Sheet 9, Follow-the-Leader Rhythm Game.

Representing Rhythm Patterns

An important mathematical practice introduced in this investigation is invented representations. If you are doing the full-year grade 2 *Investigations* curriculum, students will have had experience inventing representations in the numerical data unit *How Many Pockets? How Many Teeth?* and the categorical data unit *Does It Walk, Crawl, or Swim?*

How are rhythm patterns connected to learning math? Inventing, describing, and interpreting regular repeating patterns are at the essential core of mathematics. Students encounter number patterns and data trends throughout their math careers. Experiencing patterns physically (though actions and sounds) as well as visually allows students access to patterning in an age-appropriate and engaging way.

Why are representations important? Representing rhythm patterns develops the use of symbols to stand for something else. Second graders are already active decoders of numbers and letters. Creating and revising codes helps students move toward consistency in communicating patterns to someone else. Learning to interpret other people's representations is a useful tool for students during data and graphing experiences, as well as for future use in algebra and calculus.

In Session 1 students represent rhythms by developing their own written notation. The process of representing rhythms is a complicated one that involves selecting particular aspects of rhythm and sound from among many in order to communicate with someone else. For more information on students representing rhythms, read *The Mind Behind the Musical Ear: How Children Develop Musical Intelligence* by Jeanne Bamberger (Cambridge, MA: Harvard University Press, 1991).

Students follow these steps when representing and interpreting rhythms:

1. One student thinks of a rhythm and draws it on paper without using words in order to communicate that rhythm to others.

2. A guesser tries to act out the rhythm using body actions. If the guesser doesn't act it out correctly, the creator revises it to make it clearer. The guesser tries again.

3. If the guesser is still incorrect, the creator shows the intended rhythm pattern by acting out the rhythm with his or her body. The class then discusses what revisions need to be made to the written rhythm pattern.

This is a process that students will revisit throughout the investigation. However, in Sessions 2 and 3 students will use only three symbols that the class agrees on, creating a "code" in which a particular symbol stands for a particular action.

When first asked to represent a rhythm, students may have difficulty knowing what to do, especially since they have been asked to represent their ideas without using words. They may be tempted to draw the action itself (for example, show hands clapping) as a way of communicating a clap. Encourage students to choose a simple symbol to represent the action. Some students have used dots or x's, letters or numbers, color codes or "map keys" (see examples on p. 42). The important idea to communicate is that students are to make a representation of their own rhythm that will be clear to others.

Continued on next page

The following examples are representations for the same rhythm: slap knees, slap knees, clap, pause.

Tory shows three people in his representation. The first and second have their hands on their knees. The third is clapping. A stop sign to the right of the third person shows a pause.

Harris shows that the first two lines in each group are the same. Those represent hands on knees. The third one is darker because it represents something different, clapping. The space shows the pause in the rhythm.

Lila explains that in her drawing, F means first, S means second, 2 means twice, 1 means once, and P means pause. Because this information is not written left to right, and because we tend to read from the top down, it is difficult to figure out the order of the actions. It is also difficult to see when the pause comes because it is not marked as "third." When Lila was asked how to tell where the pause comes, she replied, "After the clap." It was obvious to her, so she did not show it on paper.

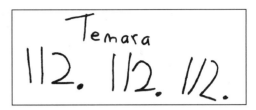

Temara explains that 1 stands for slap knees. 2 is for clap. The dot is a period, so you should stop.

Olga's representation includes some redundancies. The d stands for down, as does the down arrow. The 2 means down twice, as does the dd. For her, and perhaps for others, these lend clarity to her rhythm pattern.

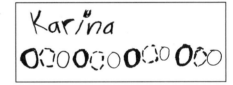

Karina uses three colors. She reports that blue (dark circle) means 2 knees, yellow (dotted circle) means 1 clap, and red (light circle) means pause. It would be difficult to interpret Karina's representation without a key. Some children might include a key in their recording.

All of these rhythm representations require some explanation because they are unique. The code students develop in the next session will function as a shared convention for your class. Like musical notation, this code is agreed on by the users and doesn't require further explanation. Struggling with these issues of communication allows students to see a need for shared conventions.

Investigating Rhythm Patterns

In this discussion, which occurs during the activity Follow-the-Leader Rhythm Game (p. 36), the class begins the investigation of rhythm patterns by talking about where they hear and see rhythms in the world around them. The teacher uses the conversation to introduce the game Follow-the-Leader.

Where do you hear rhythms?

Imani: In the rustle of leaves.

Bjorn: Music.

Ebony: Feel your heart.

What's it sound like? [*They all do it and thump their hands in time.*]

Camilla: The wind.

Temara: A horse walking? [*They make a noise together by clip-clopping their hands on their thighs.*]

[*Several students make sound effects: clapping their hands, snapping their fingers, clicking their tongues, stamping their feet, running in place.*]

Franco: Bouncing a basketball.

So sometimes you are making a rhythm on purpose, and sometimes you're running, jumping rope, exercising, or doing some other action that makes a rhythm.

I'm glad you're interested in making rhythms with your body. We're going to play a rhythm game together. I'm going to start out as the leader with an easy rhythm, and you join in when you think you know what it is. [*The teacher does: Clap, slap legs. Clap, slap legs. Students join in.*] Not everyone will get a turn, but let's have some students make up other rhythms for everyone to guess.

[*Several students create and share some new rhythms. The rest of the class joins in and follows the leader's rhythm.*]

OK, here's a new rhythm. It's not just two beats. [*Teacher does: Slap knees, slap knees, clap, pause. Slap knees, slap knees, clap, pause.*] **What do you notice about the rhythm?**

Imani: It has three beats you hear.

How about these two rhythms? Something about them makes their rhythms sound different. You need to really listen to hear what it is. [*Teacher does: (1) Slap knees, slap knees, clap, pause. Slap knees, slap knees, clap, pause. (2) Slap knees, slap knees, clap. Slap knees, slap knees, clap.*]

Naomi: The first one's faster.

I tried to do them the same speed.

Naomi: It's more.

Lila: It has like a period, and the other one just goes on.

One has a period. Do you know what Lila means by a period? It has a pause. The other one doesn't have a pause.

To see examples of students' work as they began the process of creating their own rhythm representations, see the **Teacher Note**, Representing Rhythm Patterns (p. 41).

Interpreting Rhythm Patterns

These students have been generating new rhythms, recording them on paper, and having others guess their rhythm by looking at their representations. Now they are presenting rhythm representations to the class for others to interpret. In this conversation, which occurs during the activity Interpreting Rhythm Representations (p. 40), students discuss ways to make their representations clearer and ways to show different aspects of time (fast, slow, pauses, stops, and so on).

Here's Tim's rhythm representation. Could someone else try this? How do you think the rhythm goes? [*Slap knees twice, clap twice*.]

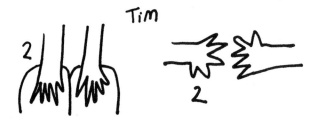

Trini: Well, it could be read that hands slap knees twice and then clap twice.

So it's a 4-beat rhythm? Any suggestions to make it clearer to everyone?

Trini: Do the pictures two times?

Like this? [*The teachers sketches. The class agrees this is clearer.*]

OK, what about Trini's representation? She drew something like this.

How might someone do that rhythm? [*Slap knees twice, clap twice*.]

Rosie: Do this [*slaps her knees twice and claps twice*] because that's like low and high.

Karina: I'd do the same as Rosie, but those are beats.

Jess: It sort of looks like down and up.

Simon: Yes, like the bottom one's like the knees and the hands are high like this one. [*Simon points to the high notes.*]

Here's another one that looks something like Trini's. This is what Jess has. What does this show?

Angel: I don't know what it means, but I would think it would be something like this. [*She claps her thighs twice, her hands once, and her thighs twice.*]

[*Jess acts out his rhythm. It is close to Angel's except that he uses pauses.*]

Jess, you're putting in some stops. Do you have a way of showing the stops? Laura?

Laura: Lines.

Where would you put them?

Laura: Between the lower notes and the high one.

Continued on next page

continued

Ayaz: I have a way to show something. [*He goes to the board to sketch what he means.*] Keep Laura's lines, but then draw an arrow back to the beginning to show it keeps going.

Here's a different rhythm that Ping is showing.

Using Ping's representation, guess what the rhythm sounds like. (Slow, slow, fast-fast-fast; all clapping) The marks are the same. What do you think that means?

Juanita: All the same action.

Lionel: I think it's slow, slow, fast-fast-fast. Because I think the *f* means fast.

Juanita: Yes, but I think there must be a wait in the middle because of that hole.

Imani: You could also say the three are fast because they're close together.

Juanita: Connecting shows faster. If they're connected they're like those notes for a recorder. They go faster because they're closer together.

The students in this class are making meaning from written symbols. Attempting to be clear about the timing of different rhythms inspires them to begin to formulate some general rules about what certain symbols might mean. A few students (Ping, Lionel, Imani) think that lines close together could show fast action (clapping). Juanita agrees, based on her experience with musical notation. Laura and Ayaz use connecting lines to show a pause. Ayaz becomes interested in showing something besides actions and pauses. He draws an arrow to show that the rhythm "keeps going." Through this discussion, students are beginning to develop ideas on which they can base the creation of a shared rhythm notation.

Codes and Conventions

Materials

- List of students' rhythm representations (from Session 1)
- Chart paper
- Student Sheet 10 (1 per student, homework)
- Students' rhythm journals
- Markers or crayons

What Happens

Some students share their rhythm representations. The class chooses three symbols to represent three actions, and pairs of students use the symbols to make rhythm representations for each other to decode. Students discuss possible rules (conventions) for representing rhythms. Groups play a game called Guess My Rhythm. Their work focuses on:

- representing rhythmic patterns with symbols
- reading and interpreting codes
- establishing conventions for communication

Start-Up

Follow-the-Leader Rhythm Game   Sometime during the day, students describe how playing the game worked at home.

Today's Number

Calendar Date *and* Number of School Days   Students can express Today's Number using doubles in their number sentences. For example, if the number they are working on is 28 (calendar date), possible expressions include: 14 + 14; 7 + 7 + 7 + 7; 10 + 10 + 4 + 4. If they are working with larger number such as 169, possible expressions include: 50 + 50 + 20 + 20 + 20 + 4 + 4 + 1 or 75 + 75 + 10 + 10 − 1. If you are keeping track of the number of school days, add a card to the class counting strip and fill in another number on the blank 200 chart.

Activity

More Rhythm Sharing

Call the class together by using a rhythm pattern that students imitate as they settle into their places for math. Begin this session by discussing two or three new rhythm representations (written on the chalkboard or chart paper) that you selected from students' work in the previous session.

What rhythm do you think this representation shows? Who wants to guess?

Students guess what the rhythm is by trying a set of actions as in the previous session. The creator may need to revise the representation after each guess to make it clearer. After someone guesses what the creator intended, ask the guesser the following question.

What in the representation gave you clues about what to do?

Repeat this activity with each different rhythm pattern.

Agreeing on Three Symbols

When people are trying to communicate, they find it helpful to agree on what certain symbols mean and how they should be written. What are some of the things we've been agreeing on? What kinds of things were we able to guess easily?

Students may be able to talk about some of the ideas they've been using—for example, that two x's mean two of the same action, or that their representations go from left to right. List some of their ideas on chart paper.

To find ways to communicate with one another we're going to play a game called Guess My Rhythm. We will use only three symbols. A symbol is something that stands for something else. For example, a plus sign is a symbol we use in math: it stands for adding.

Using symbols makes it easy to show others what actions you mean. Each symbol will stand for one certain action. We'll be making a code. I noticed that most of you used lines (or squares, stars, circles, x's) to stand for clapping. We could agree that a line means clapping and use that in our code. We'll choose three symbols that are easy to write.

Write on chart paper the title "Class Code." Then make a table with the headings "Symbol" and "Action."

Who has an idea for how to fill in this table?

Students suggest different symbols that they have been using (or would like to use) and which actions they represent. You may want to collect more than three symbols and then choose three from among those by discussing with students which ones are most meaningful to them. (Which have they been using a lot? Which are easy to write? One class chose to use an x to mean crossing hands on shoulders because of its resemblance to the shape created when you cross your arms.) Record students' suggestions in the table so that they can refer to it as they are working.

Class Code	
Symbol	Action
I	clap
X	cross hands on shoulders
•	slap knees

Encourage students to think of a simple symbol (O, +, —>) rather than something complicated such as a cat or a boat. It is best not to use musical notes, because only some students will be familiar with them, and they will have specific ideas about how the notes should be used. Waiting or pausing is not something to represent with one particular symbol at this time. This issue will become a point of discussion later in the session.

After you have agreed upon and recorded three symbols and the action for which each stands, write a rhythm on the chalkboard for students to guess. For example:

xxx|xxx|

Students can guess the meaning of the symbols by trying the actions (cross hands on shoulders, cross hands on shoulders, cross hands on shoulders, clap). Ask a volunteer to write a new rhythm on the chalkboard using the symbols in the chart for someone else to act out one at a time. A few students can act out the rhythm, then see if the class agrees. You may want to continue this for one or two rounds.

Activity

Assessment

Guess My Rhythm

Now we'll use the three symbols we've decided on. You and a partner will write your own rhythm patterns at the same time. Then you'll get together and take turns acting out your partner's code. If your partner doesn't guess it right away, give a hint by revising your drawing.

Students play Guess My Rhythm in pairs. It is helpful for students to keep the same partner throughout Sessions 2 and 3 since they will begin to develop shared ways of communicating with each other.

Students record their codes in their rhythm journals, using the pages in order and dating them. As you talk with students, encourage them to figure out how to write down exactly the rhythm they intend. They may need to invent ways of showing changing speed or pauses.

As students work, try acting out some of the students' rhythms yourself, and check with the student to see if you are correct or close.

Observing the Students This activity may be used as part of an ongoing assessment. Students will continue to represent and interpret rhythms throughout this investigation, recording their work in their rhythm journals. Keep observing for the following during Sessions 2, 3, and 4, especially for students you have questions about:

■ Can students use the symbols to record a rhythm?

■ When they act out rhythms, do they associate an action with its corresponding symbol?

■ Can you and other students guess what rhythms students are depicting?

■ Do they add clarifying symbols to their codes if someone is having trouble acting out their rhythm?

■ How are students expressing the duration of time in their rhythms? (How are students showing that two actions happen quickly or slowly? How are they showing pauses?

Class Discussion: Establishing Conventions

This discussion is part of an ongoing conversation about conventions. Conventions are rules developed by people to promote shared understanding. Reading from left to right and leaving spaces between words are examples of conventions used in our language system. See the **Teacher Note,** Establishing Conventions (p. 54), for examples of rules and issues that may arise when students attempt to establish conventions. In this discussion, three issues are raised: pausing, fast and slow, and repeating cycles. Choose several conventions for each issue. Keep in mind that students may need to try these and revise them during the next few sessions.

Gather students together in a circle with their rhythm journals and pencils. Display chart paper on which you have written the heading "Rhythm Rules of Communication." As the class decides on conventions throughout this discussion, list them on the chart paper. If your class has already agreed upon certain ideas, begin with these examples.

Everyone think about how to show this rhythm using only our three symbols: [*Slap knees, slap knees, slap knees, pause. Slap knees, slap knees, slap knees, pause.*] **Write it in your journal and then we'll have a few students show what they were thinking.**

Students' codes will look something like this: • • • • • •. However, there may be distinctions in students' approaches as they consider how to show a pause. Some may fail to show the pause in any way (• • • • • •); others may use a symbol such as p for the pauses (• • • p • • • p).

Let's look at a few examples of codes you've made for the rhythm.

Invite a few students to come up at the same time and draw their rhythm codes on the chalkboard. If they are indicating pauses in different ways, use their codes to discuss different ways of showing pausing or stopping. Students can look back in their journals to find other examples of how they represented a pause.

Were there times when you tried to show *no* sound, or waiting? How did you do that?

If students don't know what you mean, you might want to point out examples from their journals that show how long to wait using space (length on the paper or other methods). Students may have invented special symbols to represent time. Rather than leaving a certain amount of space, students may use a P or a comma for a pause, or a period or a stop sign to show a stop. Record the pausing conventions that your class agrees to on your list of Rhythm Rules of Communication.

Raise the second issue by asking students how they might show when parts of a rhythm are faster than others. Write these two rhythm examples on the chalkboard, one below the other.

‖		‖	
clap-clap	wait	clap-clap	wait

|		|	
clap	wait	clap	wait

What's the difference between these two rhythms? How do the lines show when the claps are close together in time and when there is a pause? Which claps happen fast? How can you tell?

Clap each rhythm as a class to compare them.

What do the spaces tell you? How do you know that you should clap twice quickly? What are some other ways that you tried to show that an action [or pause] is fast or slow?

Record any ideas students have for showing fast and slow on the chart. Then, using the same two rhythm examples, bring up a third issue, repeating rhythm patterns, sometimes called cycles.

How could you show that a rhythm pattern repeats? What could you draw?

Some students have used arrows to show a repeating pattern; an R to stand for repeat; or ellipses (. . .) to show that the pattern continues.

Write a new rhythm on the board with many cycles.

lxx lxx lxx lxx lxx

Do we need to show all of these symbols, or is there a way to shorten the rhythm code and still understand it?

After talking about repeating rhythm patterns, add the repeating conventions that students have agreed on to the list of Rhythm Rules. Your list might include ideas, such as those below, which have been gathered from second grade classes.

RHYTHM RULES OF COMMUNICATION

• An empty space means a pause.

• We use an arrow to show repeating rhythm patterns.

• We read rhythm from left to right.

• Use only one symbol for one action (X always means crossing hands once).

See the **Dialogue Box**, Codes, Conventions, and Pauses (p. 55) for examples of how students reach agreement on conventions.

More Guess My Rhythm

After discussing and listing the Rhythm Rules of Communication, students play Guess My Three Rhythms in groups of four. One pair of students joins with another pair.

You and your partner will play a new version of Guess My Rhythm. You will work together to draw a rhythm code for another pair of students to guess. Use the three symbols and the conventions the class agreed upon.

If possible, let partners who worked together previously guessing each other's rhythms work together as a pair for this activity, since they may have developed ideas about how to communicate. Students continue to record their work in their rhythm journals.

Observing the Students Use this activity as another opportunity to assess students' sense of rhythms in action and how they represent the rhythm.

- Are students comfortable inventing repeating rhythm patterns?

- How are they interpreting rhythm patterns?

- How are students using and interpreting the code and conventions agreed upon earlier? Do they show that a pattern repeats?

- How are students representing time? Do they show fast and slow actions clearly?

- How are they showing stops?

The physical coordination of some second graders may not yet have developed enough for them to be adept at acting out rhythms. Some may be better at expressing rhythms in other ways such as talking about them or representing and interpreting them. Others may be very good at hearing or inventing a rhythm pattern and acting it out but have a difficult time representing or interpreting the rhythm. Looking at students working together and at their written work will help you get a sense of students' strengths and areas that require development.

Note: At the end of the session, look through the representations created by pairs and select a few to use in the variation on Guess My Rhythm that the class will play in Session 4. You might wish to record your selections on the chalkboard or on chart paper.

Sessions 2 and 3 Follow-Up

Guess My Rhythm   Students play Guess My Rhythm at home with a family member. They will need Student Sheet 10, Guess My Rhythm. Ask students to write the three symbols the class agreed upon and the respective actions so they can refer to the actions at home. As a class, decide on a rhythm code for families to try. Students record this on Student Sheet 10 before going home. Remind students that the goal is to make their representation clear so that anyone could figure out the rhythm just by looking at the representation.

Follow-the-Leader Rhythm Game   Students teach Follow-the-Leader Rhythm Game to a younger class during a special visit or to a group of students at recess.

Establishing Conventions

Conventions are thought of as rules that a community develops in order to promote shared understanding. When creating rhythm representations, you and your class will need to agree on certain rules to facilitate communication.

Some conventions may seem very clear to students, because they are probably using them already (such as one symbol standing for one action), but others may be more difficult to agree on (such as choosing a way to show that a pattern repeats or considering how to show a pause).

As we read English, the cultural convention is to read from left to right. Other languages are read from right to left (Hebrew) or top to bottom (Japanese). Students may already be using the left-to-right convention in their rhythm representations, so this idea may seem obvious or unnecessary to state. However, it is useful to describe a general rule based on all the particular instances in students' work. Describing the implicit conventions of a system of communication can be useful for someone who is not yet part of the community—perhaps a student who has been absent or someone who wants to know more about representing rhythms.

Although the class has agreed on certain conventions, students may still continue to create new ones. Encourage all students to try the agreed-upon conventions to see how they work. Students often use more than one convention in one representation to show the same thing. (In the **Dialogue Box,** Codes, Conventions, and Pauses, p. 55, Carla suggests "make a big P and leave a space." Also, see Olga's representation in the **Teacher Note,** Representing Rhythm Patterns, p. 41.) What may seem like redundancy is an important part of the process of figuring out what code is meaningful.

At some point (perhaps by Session 5) ask students to use *only* the agreed-upon conventions or codes. Students may discover that they cannot show or do everything they want to with only three symbols. Or some may want to create an actual symbol for stopping rather than relying on a blank space on the page. These are interesting ideas to discuss with the full group. If other students agree that showing a particular idea is impossible with only three symbols, then the group may decide to add a fourth symbol. Keep track of the agreed-upon codes and conventions on chart paper so that they can be referred to and updated.

Codes, Conventions, and Pauses

During the Class Discussion: Establishing Conventions (p. 49), this class agrees on the three symbols representing three particular actions.

Symbol	Action
I	clap
X	cross hands on shoulders
•	hands slap thighs

Students have also begun discussing other conventions they can use to help them interpret one another's codes. They decided, for example, that the rhythm patterns should be read from left to right. They had been trying to show pauses by creating larger symbols—any of the above symbols drawn larger than the others would mean that the action is followed by a pause.

To explore the students' understanding of these new conventions, the teacher writes the following three rhythm patterns on the board.

1. x x x II
2. x x II
3. I II ••

[*The teacher acts out: 1 clap, pause, 2 claps, 2 slaps on thighs.*]

Which rhythm do you think I am doing?

Camilla: I think it's the top one. You just made a space, but it doesn't show up there. It can't be the middle one because there are only four motions there.

What would the bottom one sound like?

Camilla: The first line is not really a big line, well, actually, I do think it is the bottom one.

Jeffrey: I think it's the bottom one because it has louder and softer.

You think the big symbol means loud?

Angel: Could be the top or the bottom.

I thought yesterday that we decided that a big symbol meant a pause after it. I think what we are realizing is that we need a clearer way to show a pause. What are some other ways we might agree on to show a pause or wait?

Angel: We could use a space, but more of a space between than you put.

Like this? [*Writes* I II ••. *Angel nods.*]

Jeffrey: We could make a straight line down where we want the pause.

I am worried because we already decided that a line down means an action. It might be confusing.

Carla: We could make a big P and leave a space.

Lionel: We could do it this way [*adds dash:* I—II].

We did talk about dashes as a possibility. How about something simple like a period, a comma, or a dash? In the next activity make sure that you use a dot (•), an *x* , and a line (I) to show actions. Experiment with what works for you to show a pause, and then we will come to some kind of decision.

At this point, this class goes off to play Guess My Rhythm in small groups. (One student creates and records a rhythm on paper, and the others try to act it out.) After playing the game for a while, the teacher calls the group back together and discusses ways that students represented stops or pauses. As a class, they decide that because red lights, stop signs, and certain sounds are well-known signals to stop, they will choose two or three of these conventions for showing pauses or stops.

Guess My Three Rhythms

Materials

- List of students' rhythm representations (from Sessions 2 and 3)
- Tape or glue
- Students' rhythm journals
- Paper, 1 sheet per student
- Markers or crayons
- Student Sheet 11 (1 per student, homework)

What Happens

Students play a variation of Guess My Rhythm as a class and in small groups. Their work focuses on:

- connecting written symbols with rhythmic actions
- considering ways of showing length of time

Start-Up

Guess My Rhythm   Sometime during the day, students describe how playing Guess My Rhythm worked at home.

Today's Number

Calendar Date *and* Number of School Days   Students express Today's Number using pennies, nickels, dimes, or quarters. For example, if Today's Number is 29 (calendar date), possible combinations include: 25¢ + 4¢ or 10¢ + 10¢ + 5¢ + 1¢ + 1¢ + 1¢ + 1¢. If Today's Number is over 100, for example, 170, one possible combination is 25¢ + 25¢ + 25¢ + 25¢ + 25¢ + 20¢ + 20¢ + 5¢. If you are keeping track of the number of school days, add a card to the class counting strip and fill in another number on the blank 200 chart. For complete details on this routine, see p. 64.

Time and Time Again   Beginning on the hour, set a timer to go off at half-hour intervals. Choose a starting time and write down both the analog time (use a clockface) and the digital time. Every time the timer rings, record what time it is using analog and digital times. At the end of the day, students make observations about the data collected. For comlete details on this routine, see p. 71.

Guess My Three Rhythms

Call the class together by using a rhythm pattern that students imitate as they settle into their places for math. Use only the three actions agreed upon in the previous sessions.

Write on the chalkboard three of the students' rhythms that you saved from the previous session. Make sure they fit the conventions you've established, and use the three symbols your class has agreed upon. For example:

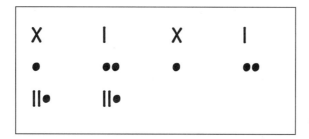

I am going to act out one of these rhythms. Follow along by copying my actions and think about which one I'm doing.

Students follow along, then stop and tell which rhythm you chose.

Which code shows the rhythm I acted out? How do you know? How could you tell it wasn't another one?

Next ask a student to choose any of the codes (even one that has already been done) and act it out. Other students watch the actions and then say which one they think it is and why.

After students have played several times, discuss the differences among the three rhythms represented.

More Guess My Three Rhythms

Organize students into groups of three. (Students may work with different partners.) Each student will need a piece of paper. Provide tape or glue for each group.

Now you'll play Guess My Three Rhythms in groups. First each group will need to create three rhythm representations to work with. Each of you can draw one rhythm on paper, using the symbols we agreed on. Make sure you draw your rhythms fairly large so that everyone can see them. Then tape all three rhythms together to make one sheet of paper.

You'll take turns secretly picking a rhythm and acting it out. The two other people in your group will copy you. Then they'll try to figure out which of the three rhythms on the paper you were acting out. People in the group should take turns being the leader.

Remind students that they can choose any of the three rhythms. If there are varying interpretations of how to act out a rhythm, students can change their drawings, just as was done in the earlier version of Guess My Rhythm.

When students seem to know the three rhythms they have been using, they begin the game again by creating a list of three new rhythm codes.

Toward the end of the session, ask students to choose one sheet with three rhythms that they think are clear and trade it with another group. If any of the rhythms seem unclear to the new group, the two groups discuss them and clarify their codes. Save these sheets in one group member's math folder.

Observing the Students As you observe students working, keep the following in mind:

- How are students using and interpreting the conventions agreed on earlier? Do they show that a pattern repeats?
- How are students representing time? Do they show fast and slow actions clearly?
- How are they showing stops?

Session 4 Follow-Up

Homework

Things That Have to Do with Time Students make a list of items at home that have to do with time, such as clocks, calendars, kitchen timers, bus schedules, and others, on Student Sheet 11, Things That Have to Do with Time. Suggest that they bring one or two of these items to school. The class will sort and discuss the items in Session 5.

Timing and Rhythms

What Happens

As a class, students look at traditional notation that shows how people represent time in music. In pairs, they compose two-part rhythm music. Their work focuses on:

- connecting written symbols with rhythm patterns
- considering ways of showing lengths of time
- interpreting traditional representations of time

Materials

- Student Sheet 12 (1 per student)
- Students' rhythm journals
- Markers or crayons

Start-Up

Today's Number

- **Calendar Date** Have students brainstorm ways of expressing the calendar date. Suggest that students use combinations of 10 in their number sentences. For example, if the number they are working on is 30 and one number sentence is 10 + 10 + 10, ask students if there is another way of making 10, such as (5 + 5) + (6 + 4) + (7 + 3) or (4 + 3 + 2 + 1) + (4 + 3 + 2 + 1) + (1 + 2 + 3 + 4). Record their expressions on chart paper.

- **Number of School Days** If you are using the number of school days as Today's Number, and the number is over 100, such as 175, encourage students to break the number into two parts (100 + 75) and then offer suggestions for how to express one of those numbers, keeping the other intact. For example: 100 + 25 + 25 + 25 or 100 + 10 + 10 + 10 + 10 + 10 + 10 + 10 + 5. Add a card to the class counting strip and fill in another number on the blank 200 chart.

For complete details on this routine, see p. 64.

Time and Time Again Students bring in things from home that have to do with time. Include digital and analog clocks as well as timers of various sorts. These items could be sorted and grouped in different ways. Some students may be interested in investigating different timing devices such as sundials, sand timers, and pendulums. For complete details on this routine, see p. 71.

Rhythms in Music: "Bingo"

Explain to students that while they were making timelines and rhythm codes, they discovered how to show time moving along on paper. They also discovered different ways to show pauses in rhythms.

Ask if anyone plays an instrument or has looked at sheet music. Before looking at Student Sheet 12, "Bingo," find out how familiar students are with written music.

We are going to be looking at rhythms in music. When people write music, they need a code to show how long or short a sound is so that the singer can sing in the right rhythm or so that the orchestra can play at the right times. What kinds of things have you noticed about how music notes look?

Students may have noticed that some notes are filled in, some are empty, and some have dots or lines next to them.

If there's a time *not* to play or sing, how does the composer show that in music?

One way composers represent this is by using rests to denote pauses in the music.

In "Bingo," half notes, quarter notes, and rests are used. Each measure (sectioned off with vertical lines) has 4 quarter-note beats. (Fractional bars appear at the beginning and the end of the music.) Half notes represent 2 beats and are indicated by an open circle with a stem, such as the notes "name," "B," and "I." Quarter notes (filled-in circles with stems) take one beat, such as each note in "there," "was," and "a." Rests (or pauses) are indicated by squiggly symbols that appear, for example, after the first "name, O." These rests are worth one beat.

Distribute the sheet music for "Bingo" (Student Sheet 12) for the next part of this conversation. Many second graders will be familiar with this song. Sing it through at least once. If students are not familiar with this song, teach it to them. Then focus students' attention on the rhythm of the song.

We're going to look at the music to the song "Bingo" and say the words in rhythm. Then we'll clap out the rhythm while we say the words and see what you notice about the different codes and rhythms.

Once students know the song, they make observations about its rhythm and musical code (notation) by looking at the song sheet and pointing out symbols that make sense to them or parts that they are curious about.

Then students clap the rhythm again without saying the words.

What else do you notice about the way the composer represented these rhythms?

How is the composer showing how long to wait? How does the composer show how long the sound lasts?

Students may notice certain notes that indicate a long time (notes for B and I) and others that indicate short times (N, G, O). They may be interested in the squiggles that are rest symbols. Clap out particular sections of the music that students comment on.

If students are interested in listening to musical rhythms, sing other simple songs together such as the ABC song. Ask them to clap and represent the rhythm using symbols. They may use one or many symbols (such as a line or an x) or even the entire alphabet (see examples below). Ask students to think about whether someone looking at their representations would be able to clap out the rhythm.

abcdefg hijklmnop qrs tuv w x y & z
| | | | | | p | | | | | | | | | | p | | | p | | | p | p | p | | |

In the next activity, students work with partners using the symbols from their class code to compose a song that has two distinct rhythms. Show students these two rhythm patterns, separated by a horizontal line.

Composing Rhythm Music

You and your partner will work together to make music that has two parts. You'll each be doing a different rhythm at the same time.

Ask for two volunteers to act out the pair of rhythms shown. Help them begin at the same time by saying, "1, 2, 3, go!"

In this piece of "music," the first person follows this rhythm: clap, clap-clap, clap, clap-clap. The other follows this rhythm: clap, cross hands, clap, cross hands. The single claps occur simultaneously. The first person does a double clap while the second person crosses arms across the chest.

Once the volunteers have successfully acted out the rhythms, ask half the class to do the first rhythm while the other half does the second rhythm. It helps students if you count (1, 2, 3, go) so they know when to begin. To help students coordinate their rhythms, you can have the first group act out the simpler of the two rhythms. The other group joins in when they have a sense of how their rhythm fits.

Show another example.

Ask students to predict which sounds will be heard at the same time.

In this case the single clap and single slapping of thighs will be heard together. There will be silence from the second person during the first person's slap.

Divide the class in half and have one half do one rhythm while the other half does the other one.

Next, students work with partners to create coordinated rhythms similar to the ones they just tried together. The rhythms should be recorded in their rhythm journals. Suggest that students draw a horizontal line to coordinate beats; one person writes above the line and the other below.

Once you've recorded your rhythm, rehearse it with your partner. Then you will have a chance to show your music to another pair.

Observing the Students As pairs are working, notice how students' written representations match the way they act out their rhythms.

■ Can partners coordinate their rhythms on paper?
■ Can they stay together as they act out two rhythms at the same time?

As pairs of students complete their patterns, have them "perform" their coordinated rhythms for other pairs. Pairs can trade music and try out each other's rhythms.

You may want to have students perform coordinated rhythms in pairs for the whole class, families, or a group of younger children, making sure to display the "music" for all to see.

If students wish to investigate rhythms further, ask the music teacher for help. He or she may be able to supply rhythm instruments or ideas on how to make them. If you are interested in extending this unit, consider ways that the content can be incorporated into other curriculum areas, such as by studying drumbeats from other countries during music or integrating the work with timelines into language arts.

As the unit ends, you may want to use one of the following options for creating a record of students' work.

Choosing Student Work to Save

- Students look back through their folders and rhythm journals and think about what they learned in this unit, what they remember most, and what was hard or easy for them to do. You might have students discuss these ideas with a partner or have students share them with the whole class while you record their responses on chart paper.

- Depending on how you organize and collect student work, you may want to have students select some examples of their work to keep in a math portfolio. In addition, you may want to choose some examples from each student's math folder to include. Items such as rhythm journals, life timelines, or Special Day Timelines may be useful for assessing student growth over the school year. You may want to keep the originals and make copies of the rhythm journals for students to take home. Consider taking notes on what you want to remember about students' timelines so they can take home the timelines themselves.

- Send home a selection of work for families to see. Students write a cover letter describing their work in this unit. This work should be returned if you are keeping a year-long portfolio of mathematics work for each student. (Inviting families to a performance of Rhythm Music or Special Day Timelines is another way to include them in their children's mathematics development.)

Today's Number

Today's Number is one of the routines that are built into the grade 2 *Investigations* curriculum. Routines provide students with regular practice in important mathematical ideas such as number combinations, counting and estimating data, and concepts of time. For Today's Number, which is done daily (or most days), students write equations that equal the number of days they have been in school. Each day, the class generates ways to make that number. For example, on the tenth day of school, students look for ways to combine numbers and operations to make 10.

This routine gives students an opportunity to explore some important ideas in number. By generating ways to make the number of the day, they explore:

- number composition and part-whole relationships (for example, 10 can be 4 + 6, 5 + 5, or 20 – 10)

- equivalent arithmetical expressions

- different operations

- ways of deriving new numerical expressions by systematically modifying prior ones (for example, 5 + 5 = 10, so 5 + 6 = 11).

Students' strategies evolve over time, becoming more sophisticated as the year progresses. Early in the year, second graders use familiar numbers and combinations, such as 5 + 5 = 10. As they become accustomed to the routine, they begin to see patterns in the combinations and have favorite kinds of number sentences. Later in the year, they draw on their experiences and increased understanding of number. For example, on the forty-ninth day, they might include 100 – 51, or even 1000 – 951 in their list of ways to make 49. The types of number sentences that students contribute over time can provide you with a window into their thinking and their levels of understanding of numbers.

If you are doing the full-year grade 2 curriculum, Today's Number is introduced in the first unit, *Mathematical Thinking at Grade 2*.

Throughout the curriculum, variations are often introduced as whole-class activities and then carried on in the Start-Up section. The Start-Up section at the beginning of each session offers suggestions for how variations and extensions of Today's Number might be used.

While it is important to do Today's Number every day, it is not necessary to do it during math time. In fact, many teachers have successfully included Today's Number as part of their regular routines at the beginning or ending of each day. Other teachers incorporate Today's Number into the odd 10 or 15 minutes that exist in many school days, such as before lunch or before a transition time.

If you are teaching an *Investigations* unit for the first time, rather than using the number of days you have been in school as Today's Number, you might choose to use the calendar date. (If today is the sixteenth of the month, 16 is Today's Number.) Or you might choose to begin a counting line that does not correspond to the school day number. Each day, add a number to the strip and use this as Today's Number. Begin with the basic activity and then add variations once students become familiar with this routine.

The basic activity is described below, followed by suggested variations.

Materials

- Chart paper
- Student Sheet 1, Weekly Log
- Interlocking cubes

If you are doing the basic activity, you will also need the following materials:

- Index cards (cut in half and numbered with the days of school so far—for example, 1 through 5 for the first week of school)
- Strips of adding machine tape
- Blank 200 chart (tape two blank 100 charts together to form a 10-by-20 grid)

Continued on next page

Basic Activity

Initially, you will want to use Today's Number in a whole group, starting during the first week of school. After a short time, students will be familiar with the routine and be ready to use it independently.

Establishing the Routine

Step 1. Post the chart paper. Call students' attention to the small box on their Weekly Logs in which they have been recording the number of the days they have been in school.

Step 2. Record Today's Number. Write the number of the day at the top of the chart paper. Ask students to suggest ways of making that total.

Step 3. List the number sentences students suggest. Record their suggestions on chart paper. As you do so, invite the group to confirm each suggestion or discuss any incorrect responses and to explain their thinking. You might have interlocking cubes available for students to double-check number sentences.

Step 4. Introduce the class counting strip. Show the students the number cards you made and explain that the class is going to create a counting strip. Each day, the number of the day will be added to the row of cards. Post the cards in order in a visible area.

Step 5. Introduce the 200 chart. Display the blank chart and explain that another way the class will keep track of the days in school is by filling in the chart. Record the appropriate numbers in the chart. Tell the class that each day the number of the day will be added to the chart. To help bring attention to landmark numbers on the chart, ask questions such as, "How many more days until the tenth day of school? the twentieth day?"

Variations

When students are familiar with the structure of Today's Number, you can connect it to the number work they are doing in particular units.

Make Today's Number Ask students to use some of the following to represent the number:

- only addition
- only subtraction
- both addition and subtraction
- three numbers
- combinations of 10 ($23 = 4 + 6 + 4 + 6 + 3$ or $23 = 1 + 9 + 2 + 8 + 3$)
- a double ($36 = 18 + 18$ or $36 = 4 + 4 + 5 + 5 + 9 + 9$)
- multiples of 5 and 10 ($52 = 10 + 10 + 10 + 10 + 10 + 2$ or $52 = 5 + 15 + 20 + 10 + 2$)

Use the idea of working backward. Put the number sentences for Today's Number on the board and ask students to determine what day you are expressing: $10 + 3 + 5 + 7 + 5 + 4 = ?$ Notice how students add this string of numbers. Do they use combinations of 10 or doubles to help them?

In addition to defining how Today's Number is expressed, you can vary how and when the activity is done:

Start the Day with Today's Number Post the day's chart paper ahead of time. When students begin arriving, they can generate number sentences and check them with partners, then record their ways to make the number of the day before school begins. Students can review the list of ways to make the number at that time or at the beginning of math class. At whole-group or morning meeting, add the day's number to the 200 chart and the counting strip.

Continued on next page

Choice Time Post chart paper with the Number of the Day written on it so that it is accessible to students. As one of their choices, students generate number sentences and check them with partners, then record them on the chart paper.

Work with a Partner Each student works with a partner for 5 to 10 minutes and lists some ways to make the day's number. Partners check each other's work. Pairs bring their lists to the class meeting or sharing time. Students have their lists of number sentences in their math folders. These can be used as a record of students' growth in working with number over the school year.

Catch-Up It can be easy to get a few days behind in this routine, so here are two ways to catch up. Post two or three Number-of-the-Day pages for students to visit during Choice Time or free time. Or assign a Number of the Day to individual students. Each can generate number sentences for his or her number, as well as collect number sentences from classmates.

Class History Post "special messages" below the day's number card to create a timeline about your class. Special messages can include birthdays, teeth lost, field trips, memorable events, as well as math riddles.

Today's Number Book Collect the Today's Number charts in a *Number-of-the-Day Book*. Arrange the pages in order, creating chapters based on 10's. Chapter 1, for example, is ways to make the numbers 1 through 10, and combinations for the numbers 11–20 become chapter 2.

How Many Pockets?

How Many Pockets? is one of the classroom routines presented in the grade 2 *Investigations* curriculum. Routines provide students with regular practice in important mathematical ideas such as number combinations, counting and estimating data, and concepts of time. In How Many Pockets? students collect, represent, and interpret numerical data about the number of pockets everyone in the class is wearing on a particular day. This routine often becomes known as Pocket Day. In addition to providing opportunities for comparison of data, Pocket Days provide a meaningful context in which students work purposefully with counting and grouping. Pocket Day experiences contribute to the development of students' number sense—the ability to use numbers flexibly and to see relationships among numbers.

If you are doing the full-year grade 2 *Investigations* curriculum, collect pocket data at regular intervals throughout the year. Many teachers collect pocket data every tenth day of school.

The basic activity is described below, followed by suggested variations. Variations are introduced within the context of the *Investigations* units. If you are not doing the full grade 2 curriculum, begin with the basic activity and then add variations when students become familiar with this routine.

Materials

- Interlocking cubes
- Large jar
- Large rubber band or tape
- Hundred Number Wall Chart and number cards (1–100)
- Pocket Data Chart (teacher-made)
- Class list of names
- Chart paper

1	2	3	4	5	6	7	8	9	10
11	12	13	14	15	16	17	18	19	20
21	22	23	24	25	26	27	28	29	30
31	32	33	34	35	36	37	38	39	40
41	42	43	44	45	46	47	48	49	50
51	52	53	54	55	56	57	58	59	60
61	62	63	64	65	66	67	68	69	70
71	72	73	74	75	76	77	78	79	80
81	82	83	84	85	86	87	88	89	90
91	92	93	94	95	96	97	98	99	100

Hundred Number Wall Chart

How many pockets are we wearing today?	Pockets	People
Pocket Day 1		

Pocket Data Chart

Basic Activity

Step 1. Students estimate how many pockets the class is wearing today. Students share their estimates and their reasoning. Record the estimates on chart paper. As the Pocket Days continue through the year, students' estimates may be based on the data recorded on past Pocket Days.

Continued on next page

Step 2. Students count their pockets. Each student takes one interlocking cube for each pocket he or she is wearing.

Step 3. Students put the cubes representing their pockets in a large jar. Vary the way you do this. For example, rather than passing the jar around the group, call on students with specific numbers of pockets to put their cubes in the jar (for example, students with 3 pockets). Use numerical criteria to determine who puts cubes in the jar (for example, students with more than 5 but fewer than 8 pockets). Mark the level of cubes on the jar with a rubber band or tape.

Step 4. With students, agree on a way to count the cubes. Count the cubes to find the total number of pockets. Ask students for ideas about how to double-check the count. By recounting in another way, students see that a group of objects can be counted in more than one way; for example, by 1's, 2's, 5's, and 10's. With many experiences, they begin to realize that some ways of counting are more efficient than others and that a group of items can be counted in ways other than by 1 without changing the total.

Primary students are usually most secure counting by 1's, and that is often their method of choice. Experiences with counting and grouping in other ways help them begin to see that number is conserved or remains the same regardless of its arrangement—20 cubes are 20 cubes whether counted by 1's, 2's or 5's. Students also become more flexible in their ability to use grouping, which is especially important in our number system, in which grouping by 10 is key.

Step 5. Record the total for the day on a Pocket Data Chart. Maintaining a chart of the pocket data as they are accumulated provides natural opportunities for students to see that data can change over time and to compare quantities.

How many pockets are we wearing today?	Pockets	People
Pocket Day 1	41	29

Variations

Comparing Data Students revisit the data from the previous Pocket Day and the corresponding cube level marked on the now empty jar.

On the last Pocket Day, we counted [*give number*] pockets. Do you think we will be wearing more, fewer, or about the same number of pockets today? Why?

After students explain their reasoning, continue with the basic activity. When the cubes have been collected, invite students to compare the present level of cubes with the previous level indicated by the tape or rubber bands and to revise their estimates based on this visual information.

Discuss the revised estimates and then complete the activity. After you add the day's total to the Pocket Data Chart, ask students to compare and interpret the data. To facilitate discussion, build a train of interlocking cubes for today's and the previous Pocket Day's number. As students compare the trains, elicit what the cube trains represent and why they have different numbers of cubes.

Use the Hundred Number Wall Chart Do the basic activity, but this time let students choose only one way to count the cubes. Then introduce the Hundred Number Wall Chart as a tool that can be used for counting cubes. This is easiest when done with students sitting on the floor in a circle.

Continued on next page

To check our pocket count, we'll put our cubes in the pockets on the chart. A pocket can have just one cube, so we'll put one cube in number 1's pocket, the next cube in number 2's pocket, and keep going in the same way. How many cubes can we put in the first row?

Students will probably see that 10 cubes will fill the first row of the chart.

One group of 10 cubes fits in this row. What if we complete the second row? How many rows of the chart do you think we will fill with the cubes we counted today?

Encourage students to share their thinking. Then have them count with you and help to place the cubes one by one in the pockets on the chart. When finished, examine the chart together, pointing out the total number of cubes in it and the number of complete rows. For each row, snap together the cubes to make a train of 10. As you do so, use the rows to encourage students to consider combining groups of 10's. Record the day's total on your Pocket Data Chart.

Note: If cubes do not fit in the pockets of the chart, place the chart on the floor and place the cubes on top of the numbers.

Find the Most Common Number of Pockets
Each student connects the cubes representing his or her pockets into a train. Before finding the total number of pockets, sort the cube trains with students to find out what is the most common number of pockets. Pose and investigate additional questions, such as:

- How many people are wearing the greatest number of pockets?
- Is there a number of pockets no one is wearing?
- Who has the fewest pockets?

The cubes are then counted to determine the total number of pockets.

Take a Closer Look at Pocket Data Each student builds a cube train representing his or her pockets. Beginning with students with zero pockets, call on students to bring their cube trains to the front of the room. Record the information in a chart such as the one shown here. You might make a permanent chart with blanks for placing number cards.

_0_ people have 0 pockets.   _0 pockets_

_4_ people have 1 pocket.   _4 pockets_

_2_ people have 2 pockets.   _4 pockets_

_2_ people have 3 pockets.   _6 pockets_

Pose questions about the data, such as, "Two people have 2 pockets. How many pockets is that?" Then record the number of pockets.

To work with combining groups, you might keep a running total of pockets as data are recorded in the chart until you have found the cumulative total.

We counted [12] pockets, and then we counted [6] pockets. How many pockets have we counted so far? Be ready to tell us how you thought about it.

As students give their solutions, encourage them to share their mental strategies. Alternatively, after all data have been collected, students can work on the problem of finding the total number of pockets.

Continued on next page

Graph Pocket Data Complete the activity using the variation Find the Most Common Number of Pockets. Leave students' cube trains intact. Each student then creates a representation of the day's pocket data. Provide a variety of materials, including self-stick notes, stickers or paper squares, markers and crayons, drawing paper, and graph paper, for students to use.

These cube trains represent how many pockets people are wearing today. Suppose you want to show our pocket data to your family, friends, or students in another classroom. How could you show our pocket data on paper so that someone else could see what we found out about our pockets today?

By creating their own representations, students become more familiar with the data and may begin to develop theories as they consider how to communicate what they know about the data to an audience. Students' representations may not be precise; what's important is that the representations enable them to describe and interpret their data.

Compare Pocket Data with Another Class
Arrange ahead of time to compare pocket data with a fourth or fifth grade class. Present the following question to students:

Do you think fifth grade students wear more, fewer, or about the same number of pockets as second grade students? Why?

Discuss students' thinking. Then investigate this question by comparing your data with data from another classroom. One way to do this is to invite the other class to participate in your Pocket Day. Do the activity first with the second graders, recording how many people have each number of pockets on the Pocket Data Chart and finding the total number of pockets. Repeat with the other students, recording their data on chart paper. Then compare the two sets of data.

How does number of pockets in the fifth grade compare to the number of pockets in second grade?

Discuss students' ideas.

Calculate the Total Number of Pockets Divide students into groups of four or five. Each group determines the total number of pockets being worn by the group. Data from each small group are shared and recorded on the board. Using this information, students work in pairs to determine the total number of pockets worn by the class. As a group, they share strategies used for determining the total number of pockets.

In another variation, students share individual pocket data with the group. Each student records this information using a class list of names to keep track. They then determine the total number of pockets worn by the students in the class. Observe how students calculate the total number of pockets. What materials do they use? Do they group familiar numbers together, such as combinations of 10, doubles, or multiples of 5?

Time and Time Again

Time and Time Again is one of the classroom routines included in the grade 2 *Investigations* curriculum. This routine helps second graders develop an understanding of time-related ideas such as sequencing of events, the passage of time, duration of time periods, and identifying important times in their day.

Because many of the ideas and suggestions presented in this routine will be incorporated throughout the school day and into other parts of the curriculum, we encourage teachers to use this routine in whatever way meets the needs of their students and their classroom. We believe that learning about time and understanding ideas about time happen best when activities are presented *over* time and have relevance to students' experiences and lives.

Daily Schedule Post a daily schedule. Identify important times (start of school, math, music, recess, reading) using both analog (clockface) and digital (10:15) representation. Discuss the daily schedule each day and encourage students to compare the actual starting time of, say, math class with what is posted on the schedule.

Talk Time Identify times as you talk with students; for example, "In 15 minutes we will be cleaning up and going to recess." Include specific times and if you like, refer to a clock in your classroom: "It's now 10:15. In 15 minutes we will be cleaning up and going out to recess. That will be at 10:30."

Timing 1 Hour Set a timer to go off at 1-hour intervals. Choose a starting time and write both the analog time (use a clockface) and the digital time. When the timer rings, record the time using analog and digital times. At the end of the day, students make observations about the data collected. Initially you'll want to use whole and half hours as your starting points. Gradually you can use times that are 10 or 20 minutes after the hour and also appoint students to be in charge of the timer and of recording the times.

Timing Other Intervals Set a timer to go off at 15-minute intervals over a period of 2 hours. Begin at the hour and after the data have been collected, discuss with students what happened each time 15 minutes was added to the time (11:00, 11:15, 11:30, 11:45). You can also try this with 10-minute intervals.

Home Schedule Students make a schedule of important times at home. They can do this both for school days and for nonschool days. They should include both analog and digital times on their schedules. Later in the year, they can use this schedule to see if they were really on time for things like dinner, piano lessons, or bedtime. They record the actual time that events happened and calculate how early or late they were. Students can illustrate their schedules.

Comparing Schedules Partners compare important times in their day, such as what time they eat dinner, go to bed, get up, leave for school. They can compare whether events are earlier or later, and some students might want to calculate how much earlier or later these events occur.

Life Timelines Students create a timeline of their lives. They interview family members and collect information about important developmental milestones such as learning to walk, first word, first day of school, first lost tooth, and important family events. Students then record these events on a timeline that is a representation of the first 7 or 8 years of their lives.

Clock Data Students collect data about the types of clocks they have in their home—digital or analog. They make a representation of these data and as a class compare their results.

- **Are there more digital or analog clocks in your house?**
- **Is this true of our class set of data?**
- **How could we compare our individual data to a class set of data?**

Continued on next page

Time Collection   Students bring in things from home that have to do with time. Include digital and analog clocks as well as timers of various sorts. These items could be sorted and grouped in different ways. Some students may be interested in investigating different types of timepieces such as sundials, sand timers, and pendulums.

How Long Is a Minute?   As you time 1 minute, students close their eyes and then raise their hands when they think a minute has gone by. Ask "Is a minute longer or shorter than you imagined?" Repeat this activity or have students do this with partners. You can also do this activity with a half-minute.

What Can You Do in a Minute?   When students are familiar with timing 1 minute, they work in pairs and collect data about things they can do in 1 minute. Brainstorm a list of events that students might try. Some ideas that second graders have suggested include writing their names; doing jumping jacks or sit-ups; hopping on one foot; saying the ABC's; snapping together interlocking cubes; writing certain numbers or letters (this is great practice for working on reversals); and drawing geometric shapes such as triangles, squares, or stars. Each student chooses four or five activities to do in 1 minute. Before they collect the data, they predict how many they can do in 1 minute. Then with partners they gather the data and compare.

How Long Does It Take?   Using a stopwatch or a clock with a second hand, time how long it takes students to complete certain tasks such as lining up, giving out supplies, or cleaning up after math time. Emphasize doing these things in a responsible way. Students can take turns being "timekeepers."

Stopwatches   Most second graders are fascinated by stopwatches. You will find that students come up with many ideas about what to time. If possible, acquire a stopwatch for your classroom. (Inexpensive ones are available through educational supply catalogs.) Having stopwatches available in the classroom allows students to teach each other about time and how to keep track of time.

The following activities will help ensure that this unit is comprehensible to students who are acquiring English as a second language. The suggested approach is based on *The Natural Approach: Language Acquisition in the Classroom* by Stephen D. Krashen and Tracy D. Terrell (Alemany Press, 1983.) The intent is for second-language learners to acquire new vocabulary in an active, meaningful context.

Note that *acquiring* a word is different from *learning* a word. Depending on their level of proficiency, students may be able to comprehend a word upon hearing it during an investigation, without being able to say it. Other students may be able to use the word orally, but not read or write it. The goal is to help students naturally acquire targeted vocabulary at their present level of proficiency.

We suggest using these activities just before the related investigations. The activities can be led by English-proficient students.

Investigation 1

morning, afternoon, evening, breakfast, lunch, dinner, activities

1. Draw pictures of a sun rising, a sun at noon, and a sun setting on the chalkboard.

2. Point to the sun rising and tell students that it is early in the morning. Explain that you are going to act out a few different activities. Challenge students to tell whether these activities are or are not likely to happen in the early morning. Pantomime and identify these activities: waking up, getting out of bed, brushing teeth, playing soccer, getting dressed.

3. Point to the sun at noon and tell students that it is noon. Talk about what happens at noon; for example, eating lunch. As you pantomime and identify these activities, ask students to tell which are likely to happen at noon: eating lunch, playing outside at recess, going to bed.

4. Point to the sun setting and tell students that it is evening. As you pantomime and identify these activities, ask students to tell which are likely to occur in the evening: doing homework, eating dinner, going outside to play, getting ready for bed.

born, birthday, older, younger

1. Show students a calendar and flip to the month in which you were born. Tell students that you will be one year older on a date in this month. Challenge them to guess the date of your birthday by asking questions such as, Is your birthday on December 4th? Is it on December 8th? When the correct date is guessed, hum the tune to "Happy Birthday."

2. The student who guesses the correct date can take the calendar, flip it to the month of his or her birthday, then let others guess his or her birth date. After each student's birthday has been identified, ask questions that require a one-word response, such as: "Will you be older or younger on your next birthday?" "How old will you be?"

Blackline Masters

Dear Family,

For the next two weeks, our class will be working on a mathematics unit called _Timelines and Rhythm Patterns_. In this unit, your child will be learning about the concepts of time and rhythm patterns.

We will begin by exploring a variety of timelines, which show sequences of events that happen over time. Students will assemble a timeline of the life of Dr. Seuss, a well-known children's author, and discuss important events in his life. Next, students will create timelines of important events in their own lives. They will also work on timelines for a special day and plan the activities to fit into 24 hours.

Students will also explore mathematical patterns expressed in rhythms. They will invent rhythms using body actions (such as clapping) and develop ways to record the actions so that others can follow them. As a class, we will develop a code in which a symbol stands for a certain body action. At the end of this unit, students will look at traditional musical notation and compose their own two-part rhythm music.

While we are working on this unit in school, you can help at home by:

- Talking to your child about the important events in his or her life. This information will be gathered one night for homework and used in class to create a timeline of your child's life.

- Mentioning what time it is at meaningful times of the day (such as what time your child wakes up, goes to school, watches a favorite television show, or goes to bed).

- Talking about ways that you keep track of time in your house (clocks, calendars, birthday cards, schedules, a kitchen timer).

- Noticing with your child how long it actually takes to do something, as opposed to how long it feels like it takes. (For a child at a party, an hour may fly by. The same hour spent ill in bed may feel like forever.)

- Listening to music and clapping out the rhythms you hear.

- Playing the rhythm games that your child will be teaching you and your family.

- Reading Dr. Seuss books together. Children will be looking at a timeline of Dr. Seuss's life during this unit.

We hope you will enjoy trying some of these suggestions.

Sincerely,

Weekly Log

Day Box

Monday, _____

Tuesday, _____

Wednesday, _____

Thursday, _____

Friday, _____

Life Timelines

Find out these things about your life.
Ask someone at home to help you.
Answer as many questions as you can.
(Some of them won't be true for you.)

How old were you when:

You first smiled? _____

You first sat up? _____

You took your first step? _____

You got your first tooth? _____

Your younger brother or sister was born? _____

You said your first word? _____

You learned to walk? _____

You learned to ride a bike? _____

You read your first book all by yourself? _____

You went to your first day of school? _____

You moved? _____

You made your first friend? _____

You lost your first tooth? _____

Write at least three other events that were important in your life.
How old were you when each event happened?

Special Day Activities

Think of activities you would really like to do at different times of day. We will choose some activities to make a Special Day Timeline in school tomorrow, so it is important that this assignment be completed and returned to school.

_____

Morning Activities

_____

Afternoon Activities

_____

Evening Activities

_____

Night Activities

Special Day Timeline

6:00
A.M.
(start)

7:00
A.M.

8:00
A.M.

9:00
A.M.

10:00
A.M.

11:00
A.M.

12:00
(noon)

1:00
P.M.

2:00
P.M.

3:00
P.M.

4:00
P.M.

5:00
P.M.

Special Day Timeline

6:00
P.M.

7:00
P.M.

8:00
P.M.

9:00
P.M.

10:00
P.M.

11:00
P.M.

12:00
(midnight)

1:00
A.M.

2:00
A.M.

3:00
A.M.

4:00
A.M.

5:00
A.M.

Events in an Adult's Life

Ask an adult at home about important or interesting events in his or her life. Record what the adult says using words or pictures. Be sure to include when each event happened.

Time Information About My Special Day

Look at your Special Day Timeline.

1. Which activities take a short time to do? _____

_____

_____

2. Which activities take a long time to do? Do not count sleeping.

_____

_____

3. What time do you start eating dinner? _____

4. What time do you finish? _____

   How long does it take you to eat dinner? _____

5. There are 24 hours in a day.

   How many hours are you asleep? _____

   How many hours are you awake? _____

Practice acting out your timeline. You might want to make a prompt sheet on the back of this paper. Write the name of each activity and the time it starts. Your list should look something like this:

   Prompt Sheet

   6:00 A.M. sleeping

   7:00 A.M. waking up and getting dressed

   8:00 A.M. breakfast

   9:00 A.M. baseball

   11:00 A.M. reading

   12:00 noon lunch

Special Day Stories

Use your Special Day Timeline to make a list of the
activities you would do and the times they start.

Time   Activity

_____

_____

_____

_____

_____

_____

_____

_____

_____

_____

_____

For homework, write a story about your special day,
and tell more about what would happen on this day!
Use the back of this sheet or another piece of paper.

DR. SEUSS TIMELINE (page 1 of 6)

Cut on the dotted lines.

0 years old
Theodore Seuss Geisel was born on March 2, 1904, in Springfield, Mass.

1

2

3

4

5

6
He saw Halley's Comet and his first owl on the same night.

7

8

9

10 years old

11

12

13

14

15

Investigation 1 • Resource
Timelines and Rhythm Patterns

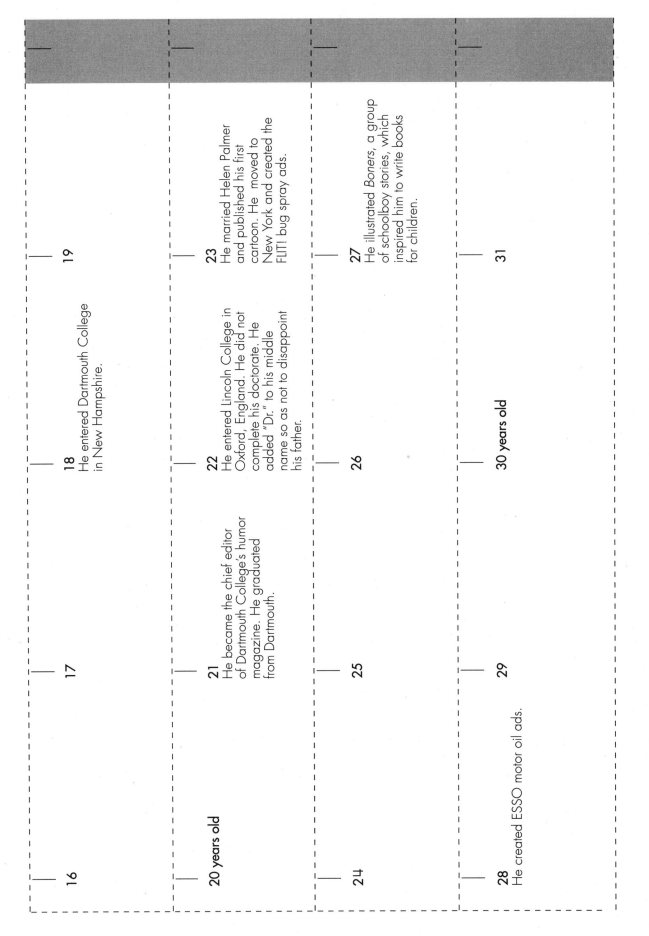

16

17

18
He entered Dartmouth College in New Hampshire.

19

20 years old

21
He became the chief editor of Dartmouth College's humor magazine. He graduated from Dartmouth.

22
He entered Lincoln College in Oxford, England. He did not complete his doctorate. He added "Dr." to his middle name so as not to disappoint his father.

23
He married Helen Palmer and published his first cartoon. He moved to New York and created the FLIT! bug spray ads.

24

25

26

27
He illustrated *Boners*, a group of schoolboy stories, which inspired him to write books for children.

28
He created ESSO motor oil ads.

29

30 years old

31

32

33
He wrote his first children's book *And to Think That I Saw It on Mulberry Street*, which was rejected by 28 publishers before being published.

34
The 500 Hats of Bartholomew Cubbins was published.

35
The King's Stilts (for children) and *The 7 Lady Godivas* (for adults) were published.

36
He became a newspaper cartoonist. *Horton Hatches the Egg* was published.

37

38

39
He became involved in making films when he joined the army's Information and Education Division.

40 years old

41

42
He received an Academy Award for the Best Documentary Short Subject.

43
He moved permanently to California. He received an Academy Award for the Best Documentary Feature, which he wrote with his wife.

44
Thidwick the Big-Hearted Moose was published.

45
He created the Ford advertising campaign. *Bartholomew and the Oobleck* was published.

46
If I Ran the Zoo was published.

47
He received an Academy Award for *Gerald Mc-Boing-Boing*, the Best Animated Cartoon.

48
He wrote *The 5000 Fingers of Dr. T*, a long feature film.

49
Scrambled Eggs Super! was published.

50 years old
He wrote the TV and radio script for *Horton Hears a Who!*

51
On Beyond Zebra! was published.

52
If I Ran the Circus was published.

53
How the Grinch Stole Christmas! and *The Cat in the Hat* were published.

54
He became president of Beginner Books at Random House publishers. *The Cat in the Hat Comes Back* and *Yertle the Turtle and Other Stories* were published.

55
Happy Birthday to You! was published.

56
One Fish Two Fish Red Fish Blue Fish and *Green Eggs and Ham* were published.

57
The Sneetches and Other Stories was published.

58
Dr. Seuss's Sleep Book was published.

59
Dr. Seuss's ABC and *Hop on Pop* were published.

60 years old

61
Fox in Socks and *I Had Trouble in Getting to Solla Sollew* were published.

62

63
His wife, Helen, died. *The Cat in the Hat Song Book* was published.

Investigation 1 • Resource
Timelines and Rhythm Patterns

DR. SEUSS TIMELINE (page 5 of 6)

64
He married Audrey Stone.
The Foot Book was published.

65
*I Can Lick 30 Tigers Today!
and Other Stories* and *My
Book About Me* were published.

66
I Can Draw It Myself and
*Mr. Brown Can Moo! Can
You?* were published.

67
He received awards for the
TV specials *How the Grinch
Stole Christmas!* and *Horton
Hears a Who. The Lorax*
was published.

68
*Marvin K. Mooney Will You
Please Go Now!* was published.

69
He donated a lion wading pool
to the San Diego Wild Animal
Park. He considered this to be his
greatest work. *Did I Ever Tell You
How Lucky You Are?* and *The Shape
of Me and Other Stuff* were published.

70 years old
There's a Wocket in My Pocket!
and *Great Day for Up!*
were published.

71
Oh, the Thinks You Can Think!
was published.

72
He received an award from
the California Association of
Teachers of English. *The Cat
Quizzer* was published.

73
He exhibited his work at
La Jolla Museum of
Contemporary Art in California.

74
I Can Read with My Eyes Shut!
was published.

75
Oh Say Can You Say?
was published.

76
He received the Laura Ingalls
Wilder Award from the
American Library Association.

77
Dr. Seuss Day was proclaimed
to celebrate his 77th birthday.

78
He received an Emmy Award
for the Best Children's Special
for *The Grinch Grinches the Cat
in the Hat. Hunches in Bunches*
was published.

79

DR. SEUSS TIMELINE (page 6 of 6)

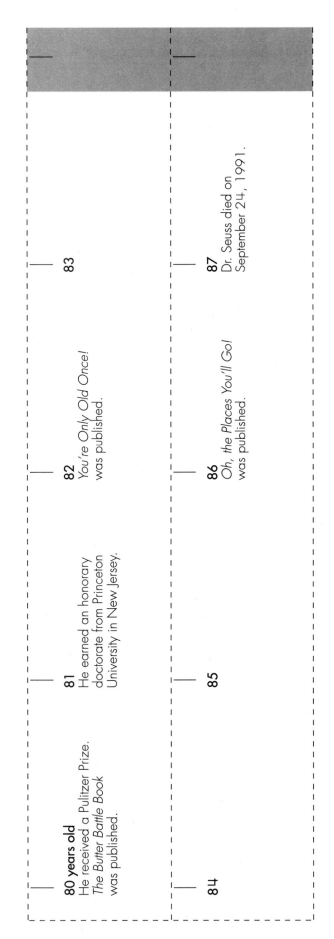

80 years old
He received a Pulitzer Prize.
The Butter Battle Book
was published.

84

85

81
He earned an honorary
doctorate from Princeton
University in New Jersey.

82
You're Only Old Once!
was published.

86
Oh, the Places You'll Go!
was published.

83

87
Dr. Seuss died on
September 24, 1991.

Investigation 1 • Resource
Timelines and Rhythm Patterns

Follow-the-Leader Rhythm Game

Teach someone at home the Follow-the-Leader Rhythm Game we have been playing at school. Record at least one of the rhythms here using symbols or pictures.

Guess My Rhythm

These are the symbols we have used to show actions.
We use these to make rhythm patterns.

Symbol	Action

Use the symbols to write the rhythm pattern the
class decided on.
Ask someone at home to act out the rhythm pattern.

Write another rhythm pattern, and have someone at
home write a rhythm pattern.
Take turns acting out each other's rhythm patterns.

Things That Have to Do with Time

Find things at home that have to do with time. Make a list of the things you find on this sheet. Ask if you can bring one or two items to school so that we can look at them and sort them into groups.

"Bingo"

There was a farm-er had a dog, and Bing-o was his

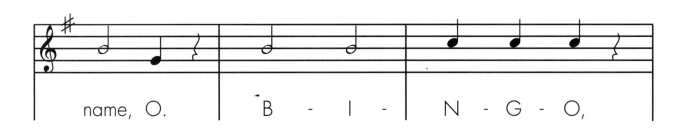

name, O.   B - I - N - G - O,

B - I - N - G - O,   B - I -

N - G - O, and Bing-o was his name, O.

Practice Pages

This optional section provides homework ideas for teachers who want or need to give more homework than is assigned to accompany the activities in this unit. The problems included here provide additional practice in learning about number relationships and in solving computation and number problems. For number units, you may want to use some of these if your students need more work in these areas or if you want to assign daily homework. For other units, you can use these problems so that students can continue to work on developing number and computation sense while they are focusing on other mathematical content in class. We recommend that you introduce activities in class before assigning related problems for homework.

Tens Go Fish   Students play this game in the units *Mathematical Thinking at Grade 2* and *Coins, Coupons, and Combinations.* If your students are familiar with the game, you can simply send home the directions and Number Cards so that students can play at home. If your students have not played the game before, introduce it in class and have students play once or twice before sending it home. You might have students do this activity one or two times for homework in this unit.

Turn Over 10   Students play this game in the units *Mathematical Thinking at Grade 2* and *Coins, Coupons, and Combinations.* If your students are familiar with the game, you can simply send home the directions and Number Cards so that students can play at home. If your students have not played the game before, introduce it in class and have students play once or twice before sending it home. You might have students do this activity one or two times for homework in this unit.

Story Problems   Story problems at various levels of difficulty are used throughout the *Investigations* curriculum. The two story problem sheets provided here help students review and maintain skills that have already been taught. You can make up other problems in this format, using numbers and contexts that are appropriate for your students. Students solve the problems and then record their strategies, using numbers, words, or pictures.

Number Strings   This type of problem is introduced in the unit *Coins, Coupons, and Combinations.* Provided here are two sheets of problems. You can also make up other problems in this format, using numbers that are appropriate for your students. For each sheet, students solve the problems and then record their strategies, using words, pictures, or number sentences.

Tens Go Fish

Materials: Deck of Number Cards 0–10 (four of each) with the wild cards removed

Players: 3 to 4

How to Play

The object of the game is to get two cards that total 10.

1. Each player is dealt five cards. The rest of the cards are placed face down in the center of the table.

2. If you have any pairs of cards that total 10, put them down in front of you and replace those cards with cards from the deck.

3. Take turns. On a turn, ask <u>one</u> other player for a card that will go with a card in your hand to make 10.

4. If you get a card that makes 10, put the pair of cards down. Take one card from the deck. Your turn is over.

   If you do not get a card that makes 10, take the top card from the deck. Your turn is over.

   If the card you take from the deck makes 10 with a card in your hand, put the pair down and take another card.

5. If there are no cards left in your hand but still cards in the deck, you take two cards.

6. The game is over when there are no more cards.

7. At the end of the game, make a list of the number pairs you made.

Turn Over 10

Materials: Deck of Number Cards 0–10 (four of each) plus four wild cards

Players: 2 to 3

How to Play

The object of the game is to turn over and collect combinations of cards that total 10.

1. Arrange the cards face down in four rows of five cards. Place the rest of the deck face down in a pile.

2. Take turns. On a turn, turn over one card and then another. A wild card can be made into any number.

   If the total is less than 10, turn over another card.

   If the total is more than 10, your turn is over and the cards are turned face down in the same place.

   If the total is 10, take the cards and replace them with cards from the deck. You get another turn.

3. Place each of your card combinations of 10 in separate piles so they don't get mixed up.

4. The game is over when no more 10's can be made.

5. At the end of the game, make a list of the number combinations for 10 that you made.

0	0	0	0
1	1	1	1
2	2	2	2

98

3	3	3	3
4	4	4	4
5	5	5	5

Practice Page
Timelines and Rhythm Patterns

6	6	6	6
7	7	7	7
8	8	8	8

Practice Page
Timelines and Rhythm Patterns

9	9	9	9

10	10	10	10

Wild Card	Wild Card	Wild Card	Wild Card

101

Practice Page
Timelines and Rhythm Patterns

Practice Page A

I read 19 books last summer. My friend Sabrina read 31 books. How many books did we read altogether?

Show how you solved this problem. You can use numbers, words, or pictures.

Practice Page B

We got 52 peaches from our peach tree. We gave 32 of them to friends. How many peaches did we have left?

Show how you solved this problem. You can use numbers, words, or pictures.

Practice Page C

Show how you solved each problem. You can use words, pictures, or number sentences.

10 + 3 + 17 =	12 + 5 + 3 + 1 =
6 + 15 + 4 + 5 =	7 + 13 + 1 + 8 + 1 =
12 + 16 + 8 + 9 + 4 =	9 + 9 + 2 + 1 =
25 + 3 + 4 + 7 + 6 =	3 + 28 + 2 + 7 =

Practice Page D

Show how you solved each problem. You can use words, pictures, or number sentences.

21 + 4 + 5 + 6 =	26 + 4 + 3 =
20 + 2 + 8 + 7 =	30 + 2 + 4 + 18 =
5 + 5 + 4 + 4 + 4 =	4 + 5 + 15 + 14 =
26 + 12 + 4 + 7 + 1 =	32 + 2 + 5 + 8 =